Faith Healing:
   FACT
? OR
   FICTION

Faith Healing:

? FACT OR FICTION

JOHN PITTS

HAWTHORN BOOKS, INC.
W. Clement Stone, Publisher
NEW YORK

FAITH HEALING: FACT OR FICTION

Copyright © 1961 by Fleming H. Revell Company. Copyright under International and Pan-American Copyright Conventions. All rights reserved, including the right to reproduce this book or portions thereof in any form, except for the inclusion of brief quotations in a review. All inquiries should be addressed to Hawthorn Books, Inc., 260 Madison Avenue, New York, New York 10016. This book was manufactured in the United States of America and published simultaneously in Canada by Prentice-Hall of Canada, Limited, 1870 Birchmount Road, Scarborough, Ontario. Library of Congress Catalog Card Number: 73-10883.

Published by arrangement with Fleming H. Revell Company.

1 2 3 4 5 6 7 8 9 10

To
STUART CHARLES ALEXANDER, M.D.
A Fine Doctor
and
A Wonderful Son-in-Law
and to
THE SESSION AND CONGREGATION
of
ST. ANDREW'S PRESBYTERIAN KIRK
Nassau in the Bahamas
*With Happy Recollections of a
Three-Year Ministry
And of Much Kindness to a
"Lame Duck"*

Preface

THIS BOOK HAS grown out of an article which appeared in that excellent religious quarterly *Religion In Life,* published by the Abingdon Press; and with editorial permission most of the material has been incorporated in various parts of the ensuing pages. The article itself was made the "lead" in a symposium entitled "Spiritual Healing," the other contributors being Prof. Paul E. Johnson of Boston University, Prof. Cyril C. Richardson of Union Theological Seminary, New York, and the Rev. Don H. Gross of the Episcopal Diocese of Pittsburgh. The symposium was widely quoted, with favor, in the secular, as well as in the religious press. It even "made" *Newsweek.*

This book has also grown out of a bitter personal experience, though I hope that I have not been embittered by it. In view of the positive conclusions set forth in the following chapters, it may evoke some surprise to be told that they were written from a wheel chair. Some years ago a "medical accident" (to put it charitably) made it necessary for me to exchange the swivel chair of my study for a wheel chair, in which, for some time past, I have been obliged to carry on my work as a minister. As may be guessed, this has sometimes been far from easy. When, at times, a mood of self-pity has taken hold of me, I have tried to encourage myself with the recollection that what has been described as "The Greatest Sermon Ever Preached" was delivered from a seated position (Matthew 5:1-3).

As a result of this unexpected and devastating blow I began to consider the problem and possibility of spiritual healing. And in

PREFACE

this quest I must include my wife, who through the years of trial and difficulty has exemplified to the full the true meaning of *helpmate*. Together we learned much about the necessity and meaning of prayer. Together we discovered how to enter more fully and understandably into the sicknesses and disabilities of other people. And together we came to the conclusions set forth in this book.

It may be urged that my own experience of not having been healed by the prayer of faith tends to invalidate our belief in the reality of spiritual healing. But over against this objection I would urge three arguments.

The first is that obviously there are limits to the operations of physical healing; just as obviously there are limits to the possibilities of spiritual healing. A man who has had a gangrenous leg amputated, or who has lost an eye in an automobile accident, cannot be supplied with a genuine replacement either by the most intense praying or by the most up-to-date medical techniques. But this fact cannot be justly appealed to in order to cast suspicion on the positive achievements—some of them apparently well-nigh miraculous—in the realms of both physical and spiritual therapy. A dead man cannot be brought back to life, not even by the most expert team of doctors. But it would be foolish to argue from this that a man in a state of shock during surgical procedure cannot be saved from physical extinction by prompt and efficient cardiac massage. Likewise a dead man cannot be resuscitated by earnest prayer, the laying on of hands, or anointing with oil (or by all three taken together). It would be equally foolish to use this fact to repudiate the cases on record in which individuals, according to competent medical prognosis, were doomed to die, yet were snatched from the jaws of death in response —so it would seem—to the prayer of faith or some other nonphysical therapy.

The second argument is that, as is generally known, modern medical and biochemical research is every day extending our knowledge of man's complex nature, and is thus increasing and improving the manifold techniques for the healing of men's minds and bodies.

PREFACE

It should also be generally known that our understanding of the nature of spiritual healing, and of the means for its accomplishment, is being gradually enlarged by the persistent efforts of consecrated individuals and concerned groups—people anxious to implement the conviction that "His Will is our Health." There are laws of the spirit, as well as laws of body and mind, and it is possible to gain increasing knowledge of the former as we are doing in the case of the latter. Indeed, we may adopt the words of John Robinson of Leyden, spoken three centuries ago to the Pilgrims as they set sail for the New World: "God hath yet more light to break forth from His Holy Word"; and we may apply them to this matter by extending the meaning of "His Holy Word" to include the revelation of Himself given in the most wonderful of all His creations, the constitution of human nature. Some light surely has been thrown on the nature and possibility of spiritual healing, and more will yet come, through the earnest efforts of those who believe that the laws of the spiritual world are as true—and as ascertainable—as are the laws of nature.

The third argument is that we must recognize that religion, as well as medicine and psychology, has an important part to play in the healing of the *whole* man as body, mind, and spirit—a fact which, despite many failures, is clearly indicated in the history of religious healing from the earliest times. There are physical ailments which, at first sight, seem to be outside the sphere of spiritual therapy, though this "outsidedness" may be more apparent than real. "Can faith mend a broken leg?" The question has been asked with an implied negative answer. Of course faith of itself cannot mend a broken leg. But if man is a body-mind-spirit unity, it is needless to argue that the spiritual factor is a complete outsider in the healing of physical sickness. And even when bodily healing does not come (as in my own case) through either physical methods or spiritual techniques, or the combination of both, it does not follow that the spiritual factor was inoperative or ineffective. As many people have found, the burden of physical disability, of bodily pain, can be borne more courageously, and a sane attitude to life be more securely maintained, when the sufferer's inner life is nourished and sustained by the prayer of faith. He can know—and quietly demonstrate—the truth of the saying:

> The answer he got to the prayer he made,
> Was power to see the thing through.

One final word may be allowed here. The master surgeon of the Renaissance was the great French doctor Ambroise Paré, usually regarded as the father of modern surgery. Before his death he prepared a volume of his case histories, published posthumously. All the way through he recognized that men's sicknesses were healed "by the grace of God and of Nature." He did not disparage his own noteworthy contributions to the science and art of surgery, but neither did he ever fail to acknowledge his dependence upon, and debt to, the divine power and goodness. He ended his record thus: "I have wanted to give these histories to guide the young Surgeon in practice, not to praise and glorify myself, but to render it to God, knowing that all good things come from Him as from a never-failing fountain and not from ourselves. By thus giving Him thanks for all good works, I pray Him to continue and to increase in us His infinite favor."

Contents

	Preface	7
1.	Healing: Man's Ancient Quest	15
2.	Healing in the Ministry of Jesus	26
3.	Healing in the Christian Tradition	41
4.	Healing in Modern Protestantism	55
5.	Healing and the Prayer of Faith	68
6.	Healing and the Reign of Law	84
7.	Healers, Healing Missions and Healing Shrines	101
8.	Healing and Human Personality	114
9.	Healing: Quest for a Lost Faith	129
10.	Healing: The Way Forward	141
	Notes	151

Faith Healing:
? FACT
OR
FICTION

1 Healing: Man's Ancient Quest

MAN'S QUEST FOR healing is as old as man himself. Indeed, it is more than likely that even primitive beasts were health seekers in rudimentary fashion. For example, the wounded animal must have licked his wounds, and the fevered animal must have sought the cooling streams, in those far-off days as in these. It is certainly safe to assume that as soon as man himself began to know the experience of ill health he tried to find some means of getting rid of his pains and maladies.

Of necessity primitive man's quest for healing manifested itself in crude and unscientific ways. What the very earliest human beings did to get rid of their diseases we can only guess. We do know that at a stage of social development not too far above the lowest levels of primitive experience man's quest for healing became closely intertwined with superstitious ideas and practices. Our savage ancestors attempted to ward off the various physical ills to which they were exposed, or to remove those they suffered from, by wearing charms and amulets, eating herbs, chewing barks, and drinking weird concoctions (including human blood).

Here we find the beginnings of a crude philosophy of human sickness. Disease was regarded as being both unnatural and supernatural in orgin. Though it was sometimes thought to be brought about by human agents (such as witch doctors) through the use of magical spells and incantations, it was generally regarded as something that did not belong to human experience as such; in this sense it was an unnatural intrusion into man's world. But it was also something decreed by angry or hostile gods or inflicted by malevolent demons; in this sense it was supernatural in its causation. In the course of time the most widespread explanation came to be that the demon or demons inflicting the disease actually inhabited, either partly or wholly, the body of the afflicted. And naturally it was further believed that no cure of the disease could be effected unless and until the demons were driven out.

This crude philosophy of the origin and character of illness dominated man's thinking for centuries. Indeed, it has survived even into our own day. There are devout people who believe that all our sicknesses come from God, even though with unconscious inconsistency they hurry to call in the doctor when they are seriously ill. And there are not a few professional faith healers (Oral Roberts is a conspicuous example) who, when they pray for the sick and afflicted and lay their hands on them, speak as if they are casting out of the bodies of their "patients" the demons who have entered in and brought about the illness.

Associated with this crude philosophy of sickness was a crude psychology. Cultural anthropologists (such as Sir James G. Frazer in *The Golden Bough*) suggest that primitive man somehow seemed to sense that there was some sort of connection between physical ills and mental and spiritual conditions. Primitive man was an animist. He believed that a living soul or spirit dwelt in every existing thing, not least in himself. It is only in recent years that the terms "psychosomatic illness" and "psychosomatic medicine" have become generally familiar. They are just new names for something quite old; and it is more than likely that every illness is, in some respect, psychosomatic (that is, possessing both physical and mental factors). At any rate, primitive man seems to have thought so, even though the concepts involved were vague to him and the language we use in this connection beyond his meager comprehension. He had enough insight into his own nature to come to the conclusion that the mental state of respect or reverence for the gods meant good health (as well as abundant crops or success in hunting), whereas disrespect or hostility towards deity brought only sickness and disaster. And surely prehistoric man would have sensed that it was a hard enough struggle to turn back invading demons without being careless about antagonizing the gods as well.

In a refined form this view has persisted all down through the centuries and survives today; that in itself bears witness that the belief contains genuine truth (indeed, what might be called *"saving* truth"). One expression of it is to be seen in revival meetings. The preacher invariably makes a fervent evangelistic appeal to his hearers to "Get right with God," adding the assurance that if they do "Get right with God" they will be free of all ills, physical as well as spiritual. "The Sinner's Prayer," used by Oral Roberts as a prelude to his spectacular "Healing Line," is a familiar example of this. Another, and different, expression of this view is to be found in the oft-quoted statement of Dr. C. G. Jung. "During the past thirty years," wrote this distinguished psychologist, "people from all the civilized countries of the earth have consulted me. I have treated many hundreds of patients. . . . Among all my patients in the second half of life—that is to say, over thirty-five—there has not been one whose problem in the last resort was not that of finding a religious outlook on life. It is safe to say that every one of them fell ill because he had lost that which the living religions of every age have given to their followers, and none of them has been really healed who did not regain his religious outlook. This, of course, has nothing whatever to do with a particular creed or membership of a church."[1]

Prehistoric man's quest for healing was, of necessity, deeply embedded in two vital factors in his experience, religion and magic. Despite some unanswered questions as to the relationship of these two, anthropologists are generally agreed that religion and magic have a common psychological root and a common psychological aim. The common psychological root is an overwhelming sense of awe in the presence of the mysterious powers of the universe, which powers being supernatural in character impinge upon man's life at every point and set the stage for all his activities. The common psychological (or should the term be "spiritual"?) aim of religion and magic is to ease the shock of life's trials and disabilities, including sickness and disease, by enabling man to come to terms with the mysterious supernatural powers which constitute his "spiritual" environment.

Nevertheless, there are marked differences in attitudes and techniques between religion and magic, even though these two vital factors were too closely joined together for primitive man to see the differences at all clearly. The characteristic attitude of religion in the presence of the mysterious powers of the universe is self-abasement; that of magic is self-assertion. Sacrifice and prayer call for humility and submission in the worshiper, whereas magical spells and incantations, the ritual dances and other weird rites, all tend to evoke a haughty self-sufficiency. Both religion and magic attempt to come to terms with the mysterious supernatural powers which primitive man felt were

Healing: Man's Ancient Quest

all around him, but not in the same way. The way of magic is one of compulsion and control; the magician aims to compel these powers to do his bidding. The way of religion is that of persuasion and propitiation; the worshiper, led and guided by the priest, would win the help of the deities through sacrificial and prayerful offerings.

Furthermore, magic tends to operate in a nonmoral context. The magician seeks to control powers which are regarded, in the main, as impersonal, anonymous, nonmoral. Religion, on the other hand, implies a genuinely spiritual enviroment; it tends to regard the mysterious forces of the universe as personal beings (like the worshipers themselves), endowed with intelligence and able to exercise free will—beings whose good offices must be won by propitiation and prayer and persuasion, suffused by humility and reverence.

Undoubtedly, our savage ancestors could not make these distinctions as clearly as we can. The primitive mind faced much that was dark and confusing; indeed, its world was "one dark, buzzing, blooming confusion" (as William James said of the newborn baby's world). In the experience of prehistoric man religion spilled over into magic, and magic spilled over into religion. And at no point was this more true than in the quest for healing. Primitive man prayed and sacrificed to ward off disease, and also to be cured when sickness came to him. For the same purposes he also cast his spells, muttered his incantations, and drank his witches' brews. And in all this the individual tribesman was led by the priest and the witch doctor, who in many instances were one and the same person.

Civilized man, no less than his savage ancestor, pursued the quest for healing. In the ancient civilizations of Egypt, Persia, Assyria, Babylonia, Greece, and Rome, therapeutic practices were devised and applied. Healing was practiced in close connection with religion, the priest and the physician often being identical. Religious rites were intermingled with therapeutic techniques. Throughout the ancient civilized world there were many healing shrines, usually associated with places of worship. The Greek god of medicine, Asclepius, whom the Romans later called Aesculapius, was a legendary physician possessed of remarkable healing powers. Many marvelous cures were ascribed to him; he was even reported to have brought dead people back to life. Temples were erected to his honor, the most important being that at Epidaurus; and for centuries these healing shrines were visited by sick people seeking to be rid of their maladies. Here the power of the god was invoked to effect the cure of disease. Frequently this was done in religious ceremonies. Often, too, the patient would sleep within the sacred precincts; sometimes he would dream that he was treated, even surgically, by the god and his assistant priest-physicians. Obviously powerful suggestion was at work, which sometimes made possible successful surgical treatment under hypnosis.

It would seem that three general therapeutic techniques were utilized, and in all three the "faith" of the patient was an important factor. The first was purely "spiritual" and made great use of prayer and sacrifice, though the edge was taken off the spiritual aspect because of the prevalence of magical notions. The second method was mental; it set great store on charms and amulets, incantations and spells (here again the magical was at work), which things set in operation the same healing mechanisms as are induced by the modern psychiatrist and psychoanalyst. The third method was physical, of which modern medicine is the lineal descendant; drugs and herbal remedies were used to bring healing to the sick body, and perhaps also to the deranged mind. And that these methods were not wholly ineffectual, that indeed striking cures were effected, is witnessed to by surviving records—literature and votive tablets.

The cults of Asclepius, which began quite early in Greek history, persisted through many centuries. But in the fourth century B.C. there emerged a "new look" as to disease and its cure. This was due to the genius of Hippocrates, the Greek physician who is generally regarded as the "father of medicine." His tremendous influence on the development of the science and art of healing, both physical and psychological, was a result of his efforts to separate medicine from superstition (although he did not manage to eliminate magical ideas entirely). He taught that good health was the outcome of the harmonious functioning of the four fundamental bodily humors (blood, phlegm, black bile, and yellow bile), and that sickness resulted when there was excess or defect of any of these humors and their consequent malfunction. Hence, good health was harmony within the organism, and ill health was disharmony. How near does this concept come to two modern doctrines—the biochemical doctrine of endocrine balance and the psychological doctrine of integration of personality!

This was undoubtedly an epoch-making idea. Before the time of Hippocrates some faint beginnings of a rational attitude towards sickness and its cure can be seen in the use of ligatures and bandages, herbal remedies and pain-killing drugs. But on the whole the realm of therapeutics was submerged beneath the waters of superstition and magic. The generally accepted belief among the ancients, civilized though they were, was that sickness came from without, inflicted by some hostile deity, or more generally produced by some demon or demons who had invaded the body of the sufferer. It followed that healing was achieved only when the god was propitiated or the devils exorcised. Hippocrates, on the other hand, taught that the origin of illness was to be found within the body (he knew nothing, of course, of the invasion of the human organism by bacteria and viruses), being produced by the imbalance and malfunction of the bodily humors.

Of course, there were defects in the distinguished Greek physician's philosophy of disease; nor was his teaching entirely free from superstition. To him sickness was purely physical in character. Mysterious symptoms—mysterious to him simply because he did not understand them—he ascribed to the interference of the gods. Hippocrates had not risen to the idea of psychological factors as the cause of ill health or as contributing elements in the experience of sickness, so he had to fall back on supernatural assumptions. He admitted that charms and amulets had efficacy in the cure of disease, but he could not explain how or why they produced their beneficent results. Thus he believed that there were other ways of establishing internal physical harmony, as well as through the avenue of the body. It was because of his genius that physical healing was given a more scientific character in ancient times, yet all unknowingly he also pointed in the direction of psychotherapy and spiritual therapeutics.

Both the cult of Asclepius and the teaching of Hippocrates found their way into the Roman world, but the Romans themselves did not make much progress in medicine beyond this. The ancient Jews, on the other hand, made distinct and far-reaching contributions to man's quest for healing, despite the fact that they shared many of the erroneous ideas of contemporary cultures. They felt little need to develop healing techniques along scientific lines; their contribution was theoretical rather than practical. The dominant feature of Hebrew thought was that of the ruling and overruling providence of

Healing: Man's Ancient Quest

God, in whose all-sovereign hands are all the issues of human life and death. He dispenses good health and ill health according to His sovereign will and purpose. This is not merely a theological concept; it is an ethical notion as well. God in His infinite wisdom and justice has conjoined the good life and good health, and likewise evil living and disease.[2] The Jews tended to believe that all sickness (and, indeed, physical disasters generally) was the result of wrongdoing, and that when the afflicted person repented of his sins prosperity would return and perfect bodily health could be expected as a gift from the all-sovereign God.

In the earlier stages of Old Testament thought this overemphasis led to the belief that for a sick man to have recourse to a physician was an act of impiety, that it was his duty to seek healing directly from God (even though priest or prophet might act as the human intermediary), and that no cure could come unless the sufferer repented of the wrongdoing that had brought about his sickness.[3]

In the course of time this exaggerated emphasis was corrected, but fortunately the ethical and spiritual aspect of human sicknesses was not obliterated. Later Hebrew thought stressed the idea that the physician was not an "outsider," but rather that he had been divinely appointed to a special and necessary function in human affairs. It was God Himself who gave the physicians their knowledge, drugs and herbs their potency, and sick people the capacity to respond to the physician's knowledge and skill. This did not, of course, rule out the need for prayer and repentance. Rather the first duty of the sufferer was to make his peace with God, by repenting of his wrongdoing, and then to call in the physician, who also should be conscious of his need of divine help.

Thus the ethical and religious note is not lost. Though medical treatment—such as was available—was not to be neglected, the fundamental requirement was that the "patient" make his peace with the deity through sacrifice and prayer and repentance. Despite all the doctor could do, no healing was possible unless the right spiritual relationship was first of all restored; but when such restoration had been effected, the inner life being calmed the physical symptoms vanished. "Here may be found a basis for the belief in spiritual healing. Religious and devotional healing seeks to bring the sick into personal relationship with God. Repentance and confession restore peace to the innermost core of the patient's being, and bodily symptoms tend to disappear in accordance with physical, mental, and spiritual laws."[4]

Ancient Jewish thinking on the problem of health and disease was not free from peculiar notions derived from their heathen neighbors; as, for example, the belief that all sickness was the result of demon possession and that it could be inflicted by sorcerers. But in its more mature aspects it had a genuinely ethical and spiritual attitude towards man's quest for healing —physical, mental, and spiritual. No better expression of this can be found than the noble passage in the Book of Ecclesiasticus:

Honor a physician with the honor due unto him for the uses which ye may have of him; for the Lord hath created him. For of the most high cometh healing, and he shall receive honor of the king. The skill of the physician shall lift up his head, and in the sight of great men he shall be in admiration. The Lord hath created medicines out of the earth; and he that is wise will not abhor them. . . . With such doth he heal men, and taketh away their pains. Of such doth an apothecary make a confection, and of his works there is no end. . . . My son, in thy sickness be not negligent, but pray unto the Lord and he will make thee whole. Leave off from sin, and order thine hands aright, and cleanse thy heart from all wickedness. . . . Then give place to the physician, for the Lord

Healing: Man's Ancient Quest

hath created him; let him not go from thee, for thou hast need of him. There is a time when successful help is in their power. For they shall also pray unto the Lord that he would prosper that which they give for ease and remedy to prolong life. He that sinneth before his Maker, let him fall into the hand of the physician.[5]

This last sentence has been translated thus:

He that sinneth against God, will behave himself arrogantly before his physician.

That is to say, having no regard for his spiritual life, he will have none for his physical.

2 Healing in the Ministry of Jesus

AN OLD PURITAN preacher was accustomed to remark that God had one Son and He made Him a preacher. An outstanding New Testament scholar, much nearer our own time, has amended this statement. Without denying that our Lord was indeed a preacher, he said, "Jesus appeared among His people as a physician."[1] This assertion is amply borne out by the Gospel records. Some people prefer not to believe this, even though they claim to be Christians. They do not take kindly to "the miraculous element in the Gospels." They have great difficulty with what are called the "nature miracles" attributed to Christ (such as the feeding of the multitude, the stilling of the tempest, etc.) and reject them completely, explaining them as natural events misinterpreted by those who recorded them.[2] But they have scarcely less difficulty with our Lord's "healing miracles." They think of Him as being pre-eminently a preacher and teacher; and they regard attempts to set Him forth as a physician as unfortunate, to say the least. They rightly set great store on "the words of grace which proceeded out of His mouth"; they give little credence to the many deeds of mercy ascribed to Him. They admit that He "went about doing good," but they deny that He performed "signs and wonders," because miracles cannot and do not happen.[3]

Healing in the Ministry of Jesus

Some of these people, in their thinking about the Christian faith, like to forget that miracles are attributed to our Lord in the Gospel narratives. They are Christians with a "naturalistic bias," who almost unconsciously close their eyes to unwelcome "supernatural" happenings. One way in which they do this is by "spiritualizing" Christ's "mighty deeds." The various physical ailments—paralysis, blindness, leprosy, etc.—were but pictures of spiritual maladies. When Jesus is reported to have restored the faculty of vision to blind Bartimaeus it is but a parable of the coming of spiritual illumination to one whose mind had been blind to divine truth; and when it is said that He touched a leper, it was but a noble illustration of His wondrous sympathy with those who were morally and spiritually contaminated.

Yet others, feeling that the miraculous element in the Gospels is a serious obstacle to genuine belief in Christ, would reduce the number of miracles to less than a fourth of the number recorded in the Gospels. They cannot regard these "supernatural events" as proofs of Christ's divinity (as previous generations of Christians did), but hold that the events themselves stand in need of overwhelming proof. In this they are undoubtedly right (the divinity of our Lord rests on more substantial attestation), but on the other hand it is difficult to see how merely reducing the Gospel miracles can be an aid to faith; for if it is possible to believe in one miracle, it is likewise possible to believe in a hundred and one. Matthew Arnold was no believer in miracles, but he put the point in a good, if somewhat flippant, illustration. It is without doubt extravagant to suppose that Cinderella's fairy godmother actually turned the pumpkin into a coach-and-six, but it is no less extravagant to believe that she did turn it into a one-horse cab.[4]

Yet others would discard altogether the supernatural element in our Lord's ministry; they argue that in the original evangelic document—that is, in the Gospel behind the Gospels—no miraculous powers whatsoever are ascribed to its central figure. These people, sincere though they may be, are a good example of the old saying that "the wish is father to the thought." Their position will not stand up to sober examination; all the evidence is against it.

On this point let two scholarly quotations suffice, one from a previous generation and one from our own. "Miracles play so important a part in Christ's scheme, that any theory which would represent them as due entirely to the imagination of His followers or of a later age, destroys the credibility of the documents not partially but wholly, and leaves Christ a personage as mythical as Hercules."[5] "The broad fact of the ministry of healing, and many of the particular incidents, are guaranteed by evidence which cannot reasonably be disputed. And the facts so evidenced go beyond any parallels from the records of modern spiritual healing. It is not a tenable position to say we will accept as credible of Jesus only such cures as seem possible to our present powers of faith healing or healing by suggestion. The confidence and achievement of Jesus certainly went beyond anything to which men have attained today."[6]

Whatever may be said against the "nature miracles" of Christ, it is certain that His works of healing are no superfluous addition to the Gospel story. Indeed, it has been argued—and not without some cogency—that our Lord's healing deeds were the great achievement of His ministry. "They were in fact the great work of his life; his biography may be summed up in the words, 'he went about doing good'; his wise words were secondary to his beneficial deeds; the latter were not introductory to the former, but the former grew occasionally, and, as it were, accidentally out of the latter. The explanation of this is that Christ merely reduced to practice his own principle. His morality required that the welfare and happiness of others should not merely be remembered as a restraint upon action, but should be made the principal motive of action, and what he preached in words he preached still more impressively and zealously in deeds. He set the first and greatest example of a life wholly governed and guided by the passion of humanity."[7]

There is one other way in which the miraculous element in the Gospels is "reduced" and that is by denying that any of our Lord's healing miracles involved the cure of physical ills. What Christ practiced was psychological and spiritual therapy, effecting the same kind of cures as have been produced by faith healers of every religion and of none. His "patients" were neurotic and their disorders were psychogenic in origin. What He cured was hysterical blindness, hysterical deafness, hysterical paralysis, etc. He restored impaired function; He did not repair damaged organs.

Whereas it may prove an aid to faith for some people, this easy way of explaining the healing deeds of Jesus cannot stand up either medically or historically. The old distinction between functional disorders and organic diseases has broken down. Recent psychology rejects it and modern psychosomatic medicine disproves it.

If the human organism is a body-mind *unity,* then it follows that sickness in one side of the unity will have repercussions in the other. Bodily disorders are bound to affect mental states, even though these effects in many instances may be scarcely noticeable; and psychological disturbances place their marks upon physical structure, even though these marks may be so slight as to be beyond detection by physical tests. If it be true that "no tissue of the human body is wholly removed from the influence of spirit,"[8] then it must also follow that what happens in the body must have some bearing upon what happens in a man's spirit (i.e., mind). It further follows that we cannot successfully confine our Lord's cures to the realm of the psycho-spiritual. No doubt, many of them did belong to this realm. It may be that the blindness of Bartimaeus was psychogenic in origin, and that the man let down through the roof by his four companions was suffering from hysterical paralysis rooted in a guilt-complex; for the blind man seems to have been cured by suggestion, whereas to the latter Christ said, "Son, thy sins be forgiven thee."

This neurotic theory of the healing miracles of Jesus does not, however, account for all of those recorded. One writer of note—who is both a medical man and a Biblical scholar of the first rank—maintains that leprosy in the Gospels was what we today know as psoriasis (which is not an hysterical skin eruption), that the woman with the "issue of blood" was suffering from a uterine fibroid tumor, and that the fever which afflicted Peter's mother-in-law was malaria. This writer maintains that these three complaints were physical disorders. They involved serious organic disturbance; not one of them could be regarded as functional, as psychogenic in origin or neurotic in character.[9]

It is clear from the evangelic records that the Gospel which Christ brought to men was a Gospel of *deeds,* and not of words only. The miracle stories are so closely bound up with the teaching and preaching that the two stand or fall together. They may not be used as evidences of our Lord's divinity in the way our fathers used them, but they cannot but be regarded as a revelation, not only of the grace of God as man's redeemer, but also of the power of God as the "Creator of the ends of the earth"—a thought which justifies the "nature miracles" as well as the miracles of healing. The cures which

Healing in the Ministry of Jesus

Jesus wrought—cures that were physical as well as psycho-spiritual—not only showed the divine compassion, they also proclaimed the *fundamental deed,* viz., that God had drawn near to man in saving efficacy. And "the nature miracles of Jesus are needed to complete the idea embodied in the healing miracles."[10]

It is quite in line with this to note that the healing miracles of Jesus were always "other-regarding," never "self-regarding." He never once used His mighty power to minister to His own wants, to satisfy His own needs. His reply to the Adversary, in the story of the temptation, is typical of His whole life and ministry. After His long and wearying fast of forty days and nights, He was famished and exhausted. "Command that these stones be turned into bread," whispered the Tempter. Our Lord thrust the suggestion from Him, though being so hungry and tired He must have felt its full force. "Man shall not live by bread alone, but by every creative word of God," He said, quoting a great Deuteronomic utterance. Thus He acted throughout all "the days of His flesh." Although He possessed mighty power, and knew that He possessed it, He was content to live as other men, relying entirely upon the ordinary operations of the world and society in which He lived. He did not call for supernatural aid as a means to escape from hunger and weariness. He faced the threat of danger and death, and shouldered ordinary human burdens, as any truly courageous man would.

Neither did He ever make use of His mighty power to confound or confuse His enemies. He certainly referred to His miracles to point up the unbelief of the religious leaders, but He never used His supernatural gift to injure them in mind or body. He could denounce, with biting invective, the blind leaders of the blind, but He did not put forth His hand nor

FAITH HEALING

speak the word to destroy them. According to the Acts of the Apostles, Ananias and Sapphira were struck dead at the word of Peter, and Elymas, the magician, was smitten with blindness at the word of Paul. But nothing like that is found in the story of Christ. Not so did He treat His enemies, not even to escape their hatred and malice. The scribes and Pharisees did not deny His extraordinary power, but neither did they fear it. They seemed to sense that He would not use it to injure or destroy them. It is true that none of His enemies was healed by Jesus. That, however, was not because of unwillingness on His part, but of unwillingness on theirs. A sick Pharisee who came to Jesus in faith and hope would have known His healing touch or word, no less than a sick publican. For the power that He would not use to relieve His own burdens He freely used to help others. If we omit the withering of the barren fig tree, then we can say that every one of His mighty deeds was done to remove the burden of pain and want and sorrow from other people's lives, but that not one was performed to secure His own comfort and security.

In one of the Apocryphal Gospels—The Childhood Gospel of Thomas, which gives a melancholy and detestable picture of the boy Jesus as a "miracle-monger"—unbelievable miracles are ascribed to the infant prodigy. Some are sheer marvels, without any sense in them, such as making clay pigeons and causing them to come to life, and carrying water in His cloak after the pitcher had broken. Some are deeds of sheer ill will, such as striking dead a playmate who had accidentally bumped into Him, and cursing His teacher, who fell into a swoon. How different from the Christ of the New Testament! He was no "miracle-monger," dazzling the bystanders with spectacular tricks of magic. Nor was any man, woman, or child hurt or afflicted by the mighty power He had at His command.

Healing in the Ministry of Jesus

"Do our sicknesses come from God?" There has been a marked tendency in orthodox Protestantism, no doubt influenced by an exaggerated emphasis on the doctrine of God's Absolute Sovereignty, to answer this question in the affirmative. Of course, ultimately everything that happens goes back to the Sovereign Will of the Almighty; hence the *possibility* of sickness must be ascribed to Him. But not the *actuality* of sickness. God wills that deep water shall drown, but not that it shall drown you. God wills that fire will burn, but not that it shall burn your house down. The *possibility* of your being drowned, of your house being destroyed by fire, is rooted in the constitution of the universe (which we believe to be the work of the All-Wise and All-Powerful Creator), but the actuality of the catastrophe is the result of the intrusion of other factors—folly, carelessness, ignorance, and it may be even sin.

Our Lord would not have said that God sends illness to men. On the contrary, He believed that disease had its moral roots in the kingdom of evil—the kingdom He had come to destroy. Never once did He tell a sufferer who came for healing that his malady was the will of God, and therefore he should continue in his pain and misery. Undergirding His ministry of mercy was the conviction that God is the author of health, not of sickness, and that when in any given case disease triumphs then something happens that ought not to happen. Is that not the conviction underlying modern medical practice? A doctor may not be a theologian—he may not even be a religious man—but he most surely believes that when he combats sickness and disease he is "on the side of the angels." His philosophy of healing is expressed in the view that Nature is the Great Healer, and that all the doctor does is to provide the conditions in which Nature can do her perfect work. And

FAITH HEALING

that surely means that there is a real sense in which good health is natural, and ill health unnatural, which for the Christian implies that the God and Father of our Lord Jesus Christ is on the side of health, not on the side of disease.

Our Lord Himself certainly thought so. "Jesus, in fact, seems to have felt towards physical and mental disease precisely as every good modern physician feels . . . in this respect He does not differ from the ordinary medical standpoint, nor can we understand Him unless we appreciate this. He always assumes that disease is part of the kingdom of evil, and never once does He give the slightest sign to the contrary. Not only does He try to heal all those who are brought to Him, but He sends His disciples forth with a general commission to heal indiscriminately. His unvarying assumption, where there are failures, is that there has not been enough faith either on the part of the healers or of the sick or their friends and neighbors. His underlying idea can only be that God is always on the side of health rather than of disease, and that where the latter triumphs, something is as it ought not to be."[11]

There is, however, one important respect in which Christ's philosophy of healing diverges from modern medical theory. He seems to have shared the prevalent theory of His day that some sicknesses, at least, were the result of demoniacal possession, and that no cure was possible in such cases unless the demon or demons were cast out. Our Lord's Jewish contemporaries had acquired this belief through their contacts with other cultures. No doubt much superstition was involved. But was there a core of truth in it? That is the question. Most educated people today—and modern medical science generally —would maintain that there is no truth whatsoever in the theory, and that it is a thoroughly mistaken view of the origin and nature of psychogenic illness.

Healing in the Ministry of Jesus

It cannot be denied, however, that this so-called mistaken view *was* held by Christ, and that He practiced exorcism. Indeed, Mark's Gospel (our earliest record of Christ's life and ministry) suggests that the casting out of demons was an essential part of the proclamation of the Kingdom of God, and the near approach of that Kingdom was proof that the kingdom of evil—to which the demons belonged—was about to fall. If the theory *is* a mistaken one, in all its aspects, then the fact that our Lord held it raises serious questions for the Christian believer. Was Christ's knowledge limited on this important matter (as it was with reference to the time of the Second Advent)? The orthodox theologian finds it difficult to admit this possibility, though indications are not wanting in the Gospels that our Lord's human knowledge was sometimes incomplete.

On the other hand, it may be that Jesus deliberately accepted a view He knew to be erroneous. He had of necessity to speak to His contemporaries in terms they could understand; and so, in this matter of demon possession, He made a concession to their mistaken ideas. Possibly He was acting on the assumption that no cure of the supposed devil-ridden patient could come about by denying the existence of demons. Mental and spiritual health cannot be restored merely by negations, as any modern psychiatrist would say. What is needed for the healing of psychogenic disorders is the positive assurance of God's love and care; and that is what Jesus gave. His work was not to raise speculative questions, but to rescue men from the power of sin, disease, and death. Admittedly, He said nothing, even in private conversations with the disciples, to correct the notion of demon-possession as the cause of sickness; and if we insist that He was mistaken, then we are left deep in our perplexity.

FAITH HEALING

But was He mistaken? Is the theory of demon-possession as the causative factor in *some* types of illness a superstitious error? Granted that superstitious ideas and practices gather around the theory, but is the theory itself unsound?

The fact that He regarded demon-possession as responsible for only *some kinds of illness* would suggest that He did not completely share contemporary ideas on this matter. It is only in the case of certain types of sickness that He cast the devils out, and this fact has to be set against the background of a general belief that all disease was the result of demon-possession.

There is a further fact indicating that our Lord not only did not share all contemporary ideas respecting demon-possession, but actually went out of His way to repudiate most of them. True, He did accept the theory that some types of illness are caused by demons, but He did not accept wholesale the popular demonology of His time (which He would surely have done were He intellectually merely the child of His own age). Indeed, in a culture that was burdened with the thought of demons and what they could do to men, Jesus seemed at pains to show that—with the exception of the causation of certain types of illness—He did not believe the theory of a devil-infested cosmos.

Dr. Leslie D. Weatherhead, who stresses both the points indicated above, quotes an authoritative word from a writer who is both a medical scientist and a Christian theologian. Jesus "commanded His disciples to gather up the fragments; thus discouraging the idea that demons lurk in crumbs. He had no faith in the ceremonial washing of hands; so repelling the notion that spirits may rest on unwashed hands. He asked for a draught of water from the woman of Samaria and thereafter entered the city; proving that He had no fear of drinking borrowed water and no belief in local shedim. He retired repeatedly to desert places and fasted in the wilderness; therein rejecting the popular conception that the waste is the special haunt of evil spirits. . . . The association of demons with animals is in conflict with Christ's assertion of God's special care over them."[12] The evidence is thus clear. Our Lord did believe in demons as the causative agents in some forms of sickness; He did not believe in a devil-infested world.

Again we raise the question, Was He mistaken in so believing? Most moderns think He was. But can we be really sure? Some modern writers—who are by no means ignorant or obscurantist—believe we may be mistaken in thinking that Christ was mistaken, urging that there may be more truth in the theory of demon possession than is generally conceded.

Here is the declaration of the famous American philosopher-psychologist, William James. "The refusal of modern 'Enlightment' to treat Possession as an hypothesis, to be spoken of as even possible, in spite of the massive human tradition based on concrete human experience in its favor, has always seemed to me a curious example of the power of fashion in things scientific. That the demon theory will have its innings again is to my mind absolutely certain. One has to be 'scientific' indeed to be blind and ignorant enough to deny its possibility."[13]

And here is the testimony of a noted British preacher and scholar, R. J. Campbell. "In discoursing upon the limitations of Jesus it has often been remarked that He believed disease to be of Satan's making, whereas we now know better. Do we? It may be gravely doubted. Here is a complex problem of which no complete solution is forthcoming by any means at our present command, but there is at least some ground for suspecting that our insight into the causes of human suffering is after all not so superior to that of the Light of the World as we have been too ready to assume. But He mistook epilepsy for demon possession. Did He? Have our wise men mistaken demon possession for epilepsy? If there be one thing almost beyond question to those who know the evidence in these days, it is that demon possession is not only a fact, but a fact of our time as well as of New Testament times."[14]

Two other witnesses may be cited on this perplexing topic. H. G. Wood, a highly competent New Testament authority, in the article previously referred to, says, "If the belief in demons be entirely illusory—a modern assumption which is seldom questioned, *though it is certainly questionable*—then Jesus was involved in a popular error." The point of the quotation is, of course, in the italicized clause. The other witness is Leslie D. Weatherhead, who has done outstanding work —both practically and intellectually—in the field of psychological and spiritual healing. With reference to demon possession as the cause of certain sicknesses, he writes, "After certain observations in the East, wide enquiry from scholars, and such study as I have been able myself to pursue during the last thirty years, I am at least certain of one thing; the matter cannot be treated in this light-hearted way. The problem is not solved nearly so easily as that."[15]

How did Christ regard His gift of healing? Did He think of it as subordinate to His power to persuade men by His preaching and teaching? Were the miracles an integral part of His mission or were they only the tolling of the bell to bring the multitudes within sound of His voice? Further, did He regard them as offering proof of His divine character and mission? Did they help His hearers—some of them, at least—to believe in Him as the Son of God?

Strange to say, these points have been warmly debated.

Healing in the Ministry of Jesus

There have been interpreters of the life of Christ who have argued that His deeds of mercy were extorted from Him, against His will, by the spectacle of human suffering. He could not endure to watch men's pains and miseries without doing something to relieve them, but He would rather have devoted Himself entirely to the "cure of souls." Others have suggested that the healing aspects of our Lord's ministry were imposed upon Him by His materialistically minded and miracle-loving contemporaries against His better judgment, and that He would much have preferred to get on with the "real work of the Kingdom." Such views cannot stand up to the evidence presented in the Gospels. That He loved to use His mighty power to heal men's bodies and minds is suggested on many a page in the record. True, He refused to work useless signs to satisfy idle curiosity, and poured scorn on those who so lightheartedly asked for them. But for Him to heal men's afflicted bodies, or their deranged minds, was no useless sign. It was rather a labor of love and compassion—indeed, divine love and compassion—in which He rejoiced. The miracles were not just the ringing of a bell. The healing touch was given, the healing word was spoken, not merely that men might be more ready to accept His message of the Kingdom, but because it was an essential part of His glorious task to lift the heavy burden of affliction from men's bodies and minds.

And yet His mighty works of healing did come as proofs of His divine character and mission. It may be that we moderns, infected as we are with the anti-supernaturalistic temper of our times, find it difficult to regard them as such. But then these deeds of mercy were not worked upon us, nor in our presence. Our Lord's "signs and wonders" belong to the historical past; and we have a right to demand to be acquainted with the appropriate evidence. We are more inclined to ac-

FAITH HEALING

cept the miracles because we believe in Christ than we are to believe in Christ because we accept the miracles. But it was different for His contemporaries. For the men and women who were healed by the Great Physician, and for those who witnessed the healings, what happened must have borne testimony to the fact that He was God's Promised One. Were not all His miracles—both "nature miracles" and "healing miracles"—the mighty acts of a Unique Personality? Did they not play some part in leading impetuous Peter to exclaim, "Thou art the Christ, the Son of the Living God," and doubting Thomas to make the greatest confession of Christian faith ever made: "My Lord and my God"?

3 Healing in the Christian Tradition

CHRISTIAN SCIENCE, which proclaims itself to be the true version of God's message to man, emphasizes the healing aspects of early Christianity. Present-day professional religious healers —like Oral Roberts, in America, and George Jeffries, in Britain—make the same emphasis. It is an exaggeration, however, to reduce Christianity to a faith healing movement, for in the New Testament spiritual redemption takes precedence over recovery from physical and mental illness, even though the faith that heals is identical with the faith that saves.

Nevertheless, it cannot be denied that Christ's original message of the Kingdom laid great stress on what is now commonly known as "faith healing." No doubt "spiritual healing" or "divine healing" would be better terms for what our Lord achieved, for the faith He demanded of His "patients" was always faith *in God*. But it was *faith* He asked for. Faith was the channel through which the "healing waters" flowed. It was the absence of faith that made it difficult, indeed impossible, for the cure to be effected. "Thy faith hath saved thee" seems to be the fundamental operative principle, either stated or implied, in all the Gospel healings. Hence the term "faith healing" is not inappropriate, and may be conveniently used side by side with "spiritual healing" and "divine healing."

FAITH HEALING

Martin Luther used to say that if the Christian believer had faith enough to be healed there was no malady from which he could not be rescued. Does that saying reflect the mind of Christ? Perhaps! At any rate, it cannot be denied that our Lord laid great stress upon faith—faith in God—as the all-important factor in His healing ministry. "According to your faith be it unto you" was His reminder to the sick people who came to be cured. Where faith was lacking healing was impossible; where faith was weak healing was likely to be delayed; but where faith existed—even though as small as a grain of mustard seed—either in the "patient" or in friends and neighbors, the miracle of healing came. Our Lord undoubtedly believed in the creative and restoring power of faith in God. "All things are possible to him that believeth."

To emphasize this truth is not to deny that other factors were involved in Christ's curative activities. His personal prestige, and the magnetism of His vibrant personality, must have played an important part in His healing work. It may be, too, that the fact that He belonged to the common people and not to the professional classes, and the further fact that His good news of the Kingdom of God drew many people after Him, were not without significance in this connection. But these were secondary factors. They were aids to faith. Their value lay in the fact that they stimulated—perhaps even helped to create—faith in the minds of those who came to Jesus to be cured.

And, of course, suggestion was involved. It is probably involved in every kind of healing, physical as well as psycho-spiritual. Every psychiatrist is familiar with the mental mechanism known as "transference"; it makes his therapeutic suggestions acceptable to his patients and so is an important element in the cure of mental derangement. And every physician

Healing in the Christian Tradition

knows that there is not much he can do for a patient unless the patient has confidence in him; such confidence enables the physician to suggest that his treatment will be successful. "It would be wholly unscientific to refuse to recognize in all healing, and not merely in these more specifically religious healings, a factor of which a materialistic and deterministic science can give no account. The very term, 'suggestion,' so commonly used as though it conveyed a complete explanation of all that happened in Galilee or happens at Lourdes, contains within itself the recognition of such a factor. For suggestion is the counterpart of faith, and faith is a personal relation and no mere psychological mechanism."[1]

This personal relationship is frequently obscured, and thus many people believe that it is suggestion as a psychological device that effects the cure. Dr. Leslie Weatherhead tells of a church member of his who, although an ordained minister, was also a practicing physician. This minister-doctor had a woman patient suffering with an inoperable breast cancer, diagnosed as such by several other physicians as well as by himself. "If ever I diagnosed cancer, that was cancer" was his emphatic testimony. His patient said to him, "Doctor, I think you may help me where others have failed, because you are a minister of God as well." She asked for medication. He knew that no bottle of medicine would save her, nor many bottles of such; but he also realized the value of therapeutic suggestion. So he gave her what in medical parlance is known as a placebo —a bottle of meaningless fluid. Within a fortnight she was back for some more of the medicine, declaring that she felt much better. In six weeks the cancer had disappeared completely.[2] Here suggestion was a powerful factor in effecting the cure; but behind the woman's belief in the efficacy of the supposed medicine was her faith in the man who prescribed it.[3]

43

FAITH HEALING

This is borne out by her remark to him: "Doctor, I think you may help me where others have failed, because you are a minister of God as well." Truly—to repeat Prof. Grensted's observation—"suggestion is the counterpart of faith, and faith is a personal relation."

It is clear that healing in the Christian tradition began with our Lord. It is equally clear, from the New Testament and from Church history, that it was not confined to Him; nor did it cease with His departure from this earthly scene. Near the beginning of His ministry Christ dispatched His twelve Apostles on a preaching and healing mission. He gave them authority over demons and power to cure disease. "And he sent them to preach the kingdom of God. . . . And they departed, and went through the towns, preaching the gospel, and healing every where" (Luke 9:2, 6). Later on He sent out seventy disciples, as healing evangelists, giving them a similar commission. "And the seventy returned again with joy, saying, Lord, even the devils are subject unto us through thy name" (Luke 10:17). Christ's rejoinder to this announcement is significant: "I beheld Satan as lightning fall from heaven. . . . Notwithstanding in this rejoice not, that the spirits are subject unto you; but rather rejoice because your names are written in heaven" (Luke 10:18, 20).

Does not this reply of our Lord underscore something which was stated previously, that in His thought and practice spiritual redemption took precedence over physical and mental healing? "The important thing for Christ was not the bodily healing, but the spiritual healing and the faith which both made the bodily healing possible and gave it its saving grace. It is very good that psychical cures should be understood and practiced intelligently; but the important thing for *faith* healing remains the spiritual change—a new belief and confidence in the power

Healing in the Christian Tradition

and reality of the love of God—on which it lays its chief emphasis."[4]

Healing by the followers of Jesus was continued into the Apostolic Age. Very soon in the Acts of the Apostles we have references to amazing cures effected by the leaders of the early Church. A number of general statements occur: "Many wonders and signs were done by the apostles" (Acts 2:43), and ". . . by the hands of the apostles were many signs and wonders wrought among the people . . ." (Acts 5:12). Of Philip the Deacon in Samaria it is said, more specifically, "For unclean spirits . . . came out of many that were possessed with them: and many taken with palsies, and that were lame, were healed" (Acts 8:7). At the Council of Jerusalem, convened to consider the terms on which non-Jews should be admitted to church membership, Paul and Barnabas reported how, on their first missionary tour, they had been enabled by God to work many miracles and wonders among the Gentiles (Acts 15:12).

But more specific accounts of healings are to be found in the story of the Apostolic Church. Some striking cures are attributed to Peter. The first of these is the story of the lame beggar at the temple gate, in the healing of whom John was associated with Peter (Acts 3:2-10). Then there is the case of Aeneas, who for eight years had been so completely paralyzed that he was confined to his bed; in the name of Jesus he was immediately healed by Peter (Acts 9:32-34). Even the shadow of Peter seems to have had curative value, probably because of strong suggestibility wedded to a very imperfect faith. Because of the "many signs and wonders wrought among the people" in Jerusalem by the Apostles, Peter's prestige was very high, and sick and helpless people were carried into the streets so that the Apostle's shadow might fall on them as he passed down the streets (Acts 5:15-16). Compare with this Acts 19:12,

45

FAITH HEALING

where it is recorded that handkerchiefs and aprons which had touched Paul's body acquired curative powers; this, too, was because of the "special miracles" God had enabled him to perform.

Some of these are specified. During his first missionary journey, in company with Barnabas, Paul healed a cripple at Lystra (Acts 14:8-10). On his second missionary journey—this time in Europe—a fortune-telling girl, presumably demon infested, was cured of her obsession (Acts 16:16-18). Some years later, when shipwrecked and cast ashore on the island of Malta, Paul healed—by prayer and the *laying on of hands*—the very sick father of one of the community's leading men. "So when this was done, others also, which had diseases in the island, came, and were healed" (Acts 28:9). Paul himself was the subject of a "faith cure." The shattering "conversion crisis" through which he passed on the road to Damascus afflicted him with what today is known as "hysterical blindness." Of this he was cured by Ananias, who "putting his hands on him said, Brother Saul, the Lord, even Jesus, that appeared unto thee in the way as thou camest, hath sent me, that thou mightest receive thy sight, and be filled with the Holy Ghost. And immediately there fell from his eyes as it had been scales, and he received sight forthwith . . ." (Acts 9:17-18). It should be noted that the Ananias spoken of here is not the same Ananias who fell dead in the presence of Peter.

There is a significant passage in the New Testament which does not refer to cases of faith healing, but to the *methods* by which such healing was to be achieved by the Church generally. It occurs in the Epistle of James, regarded by most Biblical scholars as one of the earliest written books in the New Testament. It reads thus: "Is any among you afflicted? let him pray. Is any merry? let him sing psalms. Is any sick among you? let him call for the elders of the church; and let them pray over him, anointing him with oil in the name of the Lord: And the prayer of faith shall save the sick, and the Lord shall raise him up; and if he have committed sins, they shall be forgiven him. Confess your faults to one another, and pray for one another, that ye may be healed. The effectual fervent prayer of a righteous man availeth much" (5:13-16).

This passage obviously reflects the faith and practice of the early Church, though it was probably not widespread when James wrote the epistle. For we note that he *recommends* the twofold procedure of prayer and anointing, probably on the basis of what was done in the Mother Church at Jerusalem, of which he was the head; he does not suggest that it was common practice among the churches. But that this faith healing technique eventually became widely used, and was practiced for centuries, is clear from the Christian writings of those times.

The Apostle urges that the two methods are to be used in combination, and that in the use of them church officials (i.e., the *elders*) should take a leading part as representing the whole congregation. Prayer, of course, has always been "the sword of the saints" (the phrase is Francis Thompson's) in the fight against physical and psychological ills, as well as against spiritual evils. In all the churches, and in every age, intercession for the sick and afflicted has been an important part of the church's ministry of helpfulness. All too often it has been merely a matter of form; all too often it has been not much above the level of a magical incantation. Many ministers pray with their sick parishioners merely because it is the thing that is done; many others hesitate to pray in the sickroom because of a certain feeling of embarrassment, or because they entertain the notion that it is likely to suggest the thought of death to the patient, and so increase his or her apprehension.

Those of us who are ministers of the Gospel need to re-persuade ourselves of the therapeutic value of sincere prayer.[5] Every minister should believe in the power of intercession in the ministry to the sick; many doctors do, and are not reluctant to acknowledge that fact. When we go into the sickroom and pray for the sick person—*really pray*—we ought to have an inward assurance, an intellectual and spiritual conviction, that our prayers are of great help and of prime importance. If we really pray, we will believe that; if we do not believe it, we will not really pray. In every Christian community there are people who were once desperately ill, but have regained their health and strength, in whose recovery the prayers of pastor and friends played an important part. As one discriminating writer observes: "There is some extremely good evidence, which it is quite impossible to disregard, that a certain type of prayer of an intercessory kind may have extraordinary therapeutic power. I suggest for consideration that what may be happening in cases of this kind is akin to the building up of telepathic rapport between the minds of the agents (i.e., persons praying) and the mind of the patient, resulting in sufficient stimulation of the latter to undertake with renewed energy the processes of healing and repair. The patient is helped on the mental level to help himself—and in some cases there may even be a transmutation of mental energy into physical."[6]

It seems, however, that there is some other factor involved in the answer to intercessory prayer, because patients such as infants have been healed through prayer (though it may be that "telepathic rapport" is the secret here also), as the following case illustrates. Prof. H. H. Farmer of Cambridge, tells of a mother whom he knew quite well who was informed by

Healing in the Christian Tradition

the doctors that, as far as medical knowledge could judge, her sick baby was bound to die. She asked a friend, who was a devout Christian, to join her in prayer that God would spare the child. They prayed together most earnestly, and within a few hours the child was on the way to complete recovery. The doctors all confessed to utter amazement, including one whose whole philosophy of life tended to pour scorn on "all that sort of thing."[7]

There is, in the history of the Christian centuries, and in the experience of many people today, more than enough evidence to justify the claim that intercessory prayer is a spiritual technique whereby believers cooperate with the Divine Spirit in the healing of the sick.

In recent years I myself have known four such experiences. One Good Friday an eight-year-old girl was rushed to the hospital in a very critical condition, suffering from spinal meningitis. The doctors were convinced that she was bound to die. At the Communion Service that evening I led the congregation in prayer for the child's recovery; indeed, the intercession was made a definite part of the service. Next day the child was out of danger, and in a short while she had completely recovered. The second case was that of a man in his sixties, suffering from cirrhosis of the liver. He was hospitalized for many months, with the doctors—and the patient's family—despairing of his recovery. I appealed to my congregation, on several occasions, to pray for the man's recovery. He did recover and today, at seventy, is in excellent health. The two other cases were those of women members of my congregation. One had a brain lesion so considerable that the neurosurgeon declined to operate. For some time this patient was in a comatose condition, and was not able to hear some of the prayers I offered in her presence. Again, the congregation was

FAITH HEALING

asked to join its prayers with mine. The woman is now well again. The last case was the most striking. She had three operations for malignancy, and for a long time was a desperately sick woman—too weak to eat, too weary to enjoy natural sleep. Twice the surgeon told me most emphatically that she was bound to die, that nothing could save her. Again, pastor and people joined in earnest prayer for her recovery. She was completely healed, and six years later was still in perfect health. Did prayer have anything to do with these recoveries? Without in any way minimizing the part played by medication and surgery and nursing skill, I believe it did. There seems no other way satisfactorily to explain what happened. Every minister can, I am sure, cite similar cases from his experience.

James also speaks of the method of *anointing with oil,* to be used together with intercessory prayer. As he spoke of them they were not so much separate procedures as two integral parts of one and the same method. Anointing with oil was in early centuries a widely accepted medical technique. No doubt it also had some religious significance, and in the course of time this religious meaning tended to exclude the medical reference, or, at any rate, to minimize it. We today, however, may learn something from the fact that the Apostle made intercessory prayer and anointing with oil two essential parts of one healing technique. Indeed, it is something that has come very much to the front in our time in the cures of illness, that is, the conviction that religion and medicine must act together in this important matter. There are many occasions when the doctor and minister should work in double harness, each making his distinctive contribution to the cure of the patient.

Fortunately, nowadays there is greater readiness on the part of discerning medical men to call in the minister when they think he can help, as I have discovered in my own personal experience. And it is not uncommon for interested doctors and pastors to get together in groups the better to understand their common problems, and to work out methods of more effective cooperation. But for this joint action to become as helpful as it ought to become, and as it can become, demands not only more sympathy on the part of the medical profession generally, but also a more scientific outlook on the part of the clergy. It will be to the benefit of suffering humanity when this cooperation is closer and more efficient. Meanwhile, it is good for doctors to realize that it is foolish to try to cure everything by medicine and surgery, and for ministers to know that it is just as foolish to try to cure everything by faith and prayer.

There is a third method of healing, to which James does not allude, but which has been quite common, that is *the laying on of hands*. This method has a long history behind it. Our Lord Himself used it often, and it seems as if He urged the practice upon His followers. And we see in the Acts of the Apostles that the disciples carried out His behest. But it lasted long beyond the Apostolic Age, and is being increasingly practiced today. Indeed, there are many churches—in all the major Protestant denominations—in America and in Great Britain, where Services of Spiritual Healing, in which the laying on of hands plays a significant part, are offered as an important part of the Church's program in the community.[8]

Mixed ideas are associated with this procedure. One of them is summed up in the term "vibrations"—a magic word with some people. Close physical contact, so it is believed, makes it possible for "healing vibrations" to pass from the body of the healer into the body of the patient. It seems that this is what Raynor C. Johnson means when—after speaking of the healing power of intercessory prayer—he goes on to say,

FAITH HEALING

"There is a rather different kind of healing involving physical contact of the hands of the healer with the body of the patient. I suggest here that the healing forces are operative at the aetheric level, which now becomes the level of rapport. The mind of the patient is not now involved, but the mind of the healer acts psycho-kinetically through the aetheric body of the patient to stimulate the body of the patient towards health."[9] This is probably the idea in the mind of Oral Roberts when he places his hands, sometimes quite heavily, on the bodies of those who present themselves in the "healing line." Frequently the person so treated winces, and even trembles, and often the healer-evangelist asks the patient, "Did you feel anything?" Invariably he gets the reply, "Yes, I feel something warm surging through my body," or "Yes, it's like electricity passing through me." Other faith healers find the same thing. Oral Roberts carries this "manual contact" technique even a step further, when he invites the members of the congregation to touch the chair in front of them "as a point of contact."

This interpretation of the laying on of hands has a kinship with the theory of magnetic fluid, associated chiefly with the German physician, Franz Anton Mesmer. This magnetic fluid, we are told, "is an emanation from ourselves guided by the will.... He who magnetizes for curative purposes is aiding with his own life the failing life of the sufferer." How far is that from the manual contact theory of healing as understood by some contemporary healers? Whether it be true or not, there is no evidence that our Lord, or His immediate followers, thought thus when they laid their hands on the sick.

A more valid, and certainly a more helpful, idea is that the laying on of hands symbolizes human sympathy, and identity of purpose between the healer and the patient. The procedure is no mere mechanical rite, operating as a matter of course,

Healing in the Christian Tradition

but a sign and seal of the love of God brought to bear on human life. Physical contiguity of itself is nothing; its value lies in what it sets forth as to the relationship between human suffering and the divine compassion. If the healer is the medium or channel through which God's healing power flows, then the touch of the healer is an assurance of that fact to the one who desires to be healed. That is why the laying on of hands is often spoken of as the "Sacrament of Healing." And that is why for several centuries it played an important part in the Church's ministry to the sick.

That ministry has been carried on for centuries, but not always on the highest levels of thought. It has been argued by some that in the Apostolic Age there was a distinct descent, in this matter of healing, from the outlook and achievement of the Master Healer, that the successes of the immediate followers of Christ were due more to the power of psychological suggestibility in the people than to genuine spiritual power in the Apostles. It is a debatable point. It is certain, however, that in the succeeding centuries the Church's healing program and techniques and ideas did drop to a very low level. Some of it was genuinely sacramental, and much energy, time, and skill were expended on the care of the sick and afflicted. But unfortunately many superstitious ideas gravitated to the Church's concern for suffering humanity. Spiritual offices became overlaid with magical notions and practices. For example, it was recommended that the anointing of the sick be done with oil taken from a martyr's tomb. Another practice was to mix oil, water, and dust from the scene of a martyrdom. By these and other means cures were effected, and these were exaggerated into miracles on a level with those recorded in the New Testament. Magical efficacy rather than spiritual significance seemed to be the dominant characteristic; and this was conjoined with frequent opposition to anything in the nature of quasi-scientific medicine and surgery. By the end of the Middle Ages the Church had amassed a vast body of material—much of it associated with deceased saints—under the heading of faith healing in particular and miracles in general.[10]

4 Healing in Modern Protestantism

UNTIL QUITE RECENT times Protestantism generally has been strongly inclined to discredit faith healing, and for the most part non-Catholic Christians have relied upon orthodox medicine for the cure of sickness. Of course, Catholics, too, accept the good offices of the doctor and surgeon (not a few of whom themselves are Catholics); but the readiness with which the "good Catholic" believes the stories of miracles, both healings and others, from the Church's past creates in him a favorable "mental set" toward the phenomena of Lourdes in France, St. Anne de Beaupré in Quebec, Canada, and other such shrines.

Protestants, on the other hand, have tended to be suspicious of anything that seemed to savor of the miraculous, partly because of historic Protestantism's repudiation of the "cult of the saints." It is also likely that the Calvinistic insistence upon the Absolute Sovereignty of God—God as Arbitrary Will—had considerable, though subtle, influence in creating Protestantism's widespread disregard of spiritual therapeutics. For the tendency among the followers of John Calvin (and they were very many) would be to accept sickness as the will of heaven, and therefore as something to be endured rather than cured; though, no doubt even the early Calvinists, being human, sought the aid of the physician when sick. No wonder the Jewish philosopher, Spinoza, referred scornfully to "that last asylum of ignorance, the will of God"! Nevertheless, there were some early Protestants who were not hostile to faith healing ideas and practices. Martin Luther, for example, believed that healing by faith was possible, and put his conviction to the test when his friend and fellow-reformer, Philip Melanchthon, was sick. The Moravians and the early Methodists also accepted faith healing by prayer; with them, as with Luther, it was freed for the most part from magical ideas (though the founder of the Methodists, John Wesley, believed in the reality of witchcraft).

The negative attitude of Protestantism generally to spiritual therapeutics proved unsatisfactory, and was bound to produce a reaction in the opposite direction. It was almost inevitable that developments should take place, even movements arise, more or less Christian, to correct the balance and awaken faith in the possibility of religious or spiritual healing.

During the past three centuries striking instances of spiritual healing have appeared within most of the Protestant denominations. The cures, however, were unorthodox, achieved by unorthodox methods, and were looked askance at by Church people at large. They were not officially recognized, and the healers themselves were regarded with suspicion by their fellow Protestants and vigorously opposed by the medical profession. The chief method used was intercessory prayer; frequently manual contact and oil anointing were used as subsidiary procedures. Many cures took place at revivalist meetings. Even John Wesley—who regarded *all* sickness the result of demon possession—claimed several successes in casting out the devils.

George Fox, the Quaker, was an early Protestant spiritual healer, and in his *Journal* recorded healings he claimed were

Healing in Modern Protestantism

the result of his instrumentality. A contemporary of Fox was an Irish Protestant with the very un-Irish name of Valentine Greatrakes. He became famous throughout England as a healer of rheumatic and other ailments by means of the laying on of hands; and many of the most noted men of the time believed in him and praised his powers.

Since the beginning of the nineteenth century there have risen other individuals and groups devoted to healing by spiritual means. Joseph Smith, the founder of the Church of the Latter Day Saints (Mormons), claimed successes as a faith healer. He and his fellow Mormons used magical methods, such as holy handkerchiefs, and maintained that even broken bones were suddenly mended by these means. A healing-evangelist who achieved considerable fame in America was a clergyman named G. O. Barnes. He went all over the country holding successful healing services, thus anticipating Oral Roberts (but without the aid of radio and television). Towards the end of the century the country was stirred by J. Alexander Dowie, who founded the Christian Catholic Apostolic Church in Chicago. He claims to have been a weak and puny young man, but in answer to earnest prayer God made him strong and vigorous (so he proclaimed) and sent him forth to heal.[1]

Looking back it is easy to see that there was a kind of spiritual vacuum in the Church's ministry to human need, and faith healing movements sprang up to fill the vacuum. The most important, and best known of them all, is of course what is known as Christian Science, founded by a remarkable woman, Mrs. Mary Baker Eddy, through whose insight into human need and through whose organizing genius a coherent and vital church has been established and developed. It has been said that Christian Science makes a religion of healing and healing of religion, a criticism which the followers of

FAITH HEALING

Mrs. Eddy are inclined to resent, maintaining that there is much more in Christian Science than that. There *is* much more in Christian Science than healing; nevertheless, the healing part of the system is most important; indeed, it is that aspect which gives Christian Science its popular appeal and first attracts people and makes converts.

It insists upon "the power of positive thinking,"[2] which is a good thing within the limits of sanity and sound sense. And its proclamation that God is All-Love and All-Goodness (a thought not much in evidence in the orthodox Christianity of Mrs. Baker Eddy's day) came to very many people as indeed the "good news" of the Gospel, lifting the sick and suffering up to new levels of bodily health and spiritual peace.

On this point we may quote the personal testimony of Erwin Canham, the highly respected editor of *The Christian Science Monitor*. His mother was a very sick woman; his father, a restless, aimless, troubled and insecure man. There was no focal point in the family; its members lived in an atmosphere of spiritual gloom and low visibility. "Then disaster struck," writes Mr. Canham. "My mother became seriously ill with constricting tumors, or other growths, in her throat, and the medical diagnosis was forbidding. Doctors said they could do nothing for her." Mrs. Canham had read something about Christian Science, and feeling herself near to death's door she asked her family to get the services of a Christian Science practitioner. One was contacted over a hundred miles away, and she was asked by phone to give Mrs. Canham "absent treatment" since the practitioner and the patient could not be brought together.

"Treatment, we learned, is prayer," continues Mr. Canham, "prayer used in the manner of the request made to Jesus by the centurion (Matthew 8: 5-10). Jesus, on this occasion, agreed to go to the sick man's home, but the centurion said it was not necessary; he knew if Jesus said it would be so, it would be accomplished. 'And Jesus said unto the centurion, Go thy way; and as thou hast believed, so be it done unto thee. And his servant was healed in the self-same hour.' Across the distances, then, we joined in prayer. We prayed, we prayed hard.... My mother was completely healed. From then until her passing, nearly forty years later, my mother enjoyed the most radiant good health. That morning, my father's life changed too. Imbued with this new possibility of spiritual healing, he derived from my mother's experience the strength which was to conquer all the problems that faced us. Suddenly his life began to take on direction and purpose, which he never again lost."

Erwin Canham adds to this account a note about himself. "Naturally I was vividly aware of the change in my family, and in myself. My own sickly boyhood turned into a vigorous and healthy life, and I do not recall a single moment when I was prevented, by sickness, from meeting whatever responsibilities faced me."[3]

Many testimonies like that of the editor of *The Christian Science Monitor* have been given, and more will be given, by the followers of Mrs. Baker Eddy. Their number and character are impressive. Their witness to the healing potentiality and achievement of the Christian Science movement cannot be lightly set aside. But the philosophy upon which the movement is based, in which it is rooted, and by which it is permeated, is difficult for many people to accept.

Yet the central principle of the Christian Science point of view is simple and direct. It affirms: All is Spirit. There is no such thing as matter, for all is Mind. Therefore, there is no such thing as body. Sickness does not exist, since there is no body in which it can exist. Body and disease belong to the realm of "mortal error." So then the way to health is the denial that disease exists. When people are sick and in pain it is because they are victims of "mortal error," and if they will but throw off the "mortal error" they will be perfectly healthy.

And what about the fact of death? Christian Scientists do not normally speak of death (though *The Christian Science Monitor* cannot escape the word in its news columns); they prefer to speak of "passing." But a camouflage term cannot alter the reality of death. Christian Scientists die, when their time comes, like the rest of us; and it is just as much a matter of painful sorrow to their bereaved friends and relatives as it is in the case of those who are "outside the fold." But if disease is a nonreality because of the belief in "mortal error," then the death of the body as the outcome of disease (or from any other cause) must likewise be a nonreality. The Christian Science technique may be able to cure its adherents of pain and sickness, but it cannot cure them of that which brings our earthly life to an end. "All men are mortal" is an old saying, profoundly true; the followers of Mrs. Eddy, however healthful they may be during their span of life, are not excluded from its universality. Eventually they die like the rest of mankind. Even the founder of this system had to "shuffle off this mortal coil."

It is natural that the reaction of orthodox churches to the Christian Science movement should be one of denial and negation, suspicion of the reality of the cures claimed and repudiation of what was regarded as a travesty of the Gospel of Christ. But at the beginning of our century there was a recognition of the place of spiritual healing in the Church's ministry to human need, and an attempt to bring religion and medicine together in seeking to cure human ills. In 1905 two American clergymen, Elwood Worcester and Samuel McComb, initiated in Boston what came to be popularly known as the Emmanuel Movement (since changed to the Craigie Foundation), in

Healing in Modern Protestantism

which they had the sympathy and active support of many members of the medical profession.[4] In his introduction to *Body, Mind and Spirit* (of which he was the joint author with Dr. McComb) Dr. Worcester wrote: "What distinguishes this work from all healing cults known to me is its frank recognition of Religion and Science as the great controlling forces of human life and the attempt to bring these two highest creations of man into relations of helpful cooperation.... To the combination of these motives, the scientific and the spiritual, I ascribe what I may or may not be pardoned for regarding as the superiority of our results and the permanence of improvement in innumerable cases which had found no relief through other modes of treatment.... From the beginning we have associated ourselves with competent medical men and surgeons. Indeed, had such cooperation been refused, I should not have dreamed of assuming responsibility for the sick in mind and body. For many years most of our patients have been sent to us by physicians, and in all cases which involved more than the need of moral and spiritual advice we have left no stone unturned to procure the best diagnosis and medical care obtainable.... In other words, we have truly honored the physician and the science and art of medicine."[5]

In the same year the Emmanuel Movement began in New England a similar venture was started in Great Britain. It was called The Guild of Health and was initiated by three Anglican clergymen, Percy Dearmer, Harold Anson, and Conrad Noel. It was not confined to the Church of England. It sought —and still seeks—to unite all the churches in an organization having no official connection with any one denomination. Its watchword is "Abundant Life," and it recognizes that in the quest for this both religion and medicine have their important parts to play. Its own statement of faith reads, "The Guild of

FAITH HEALING

Health is a Christian Society engaged in seeking to recapture and proclaim the secret of abundant physical, mental and spiritual life, such as was demonstrated in the ministry of Jesus Christ and His Apostles. The Guild believes the Christian Faith to be a religion 'of power, of love and of a sound mind' which comes to sick people with the healing touch of strength and truth and love. We seek to proclaim the power of this truth to transform the lives of all who yield to it—alike in body, mind and spirit."[6] In pursuing this aim the Guild accepts the skills and techniques as divine endowments, and adds to them the specifically religious procedures of intercessory prayer, anointing with oil, and the laying on of hands.

Other societies having much the same aim and philosophy as the Guild of Health have arisen in our day, such as the Guild of St. Raphael (which is confined to the Anglican Church); the Divine Healing Mission of the late James Moore Hickson (which was predominantly Anglican), in which little emphasis is placed on medical help; the Methodist Society for Medical and Pastoral Practice; and the Friends' Spiritual Healing Fellowship. In 1944 the late Archbishop Temple inaugurated the Churches' Council of Healing, its purpose being to consider the whole problem of spiritual healing, and to promote the closest possible cooperation between doctors and clergy. This purpose secured the approval of the Council of the British Medical Association, which asserted that "there is no ethical reason to prevent medical practitioners from cooperating with the clergy in all cases, and more especially those in which the doctor in charge of the patient thinks that religious ministrations will conduce to health and peace of mind or lead to recovery."[7]

In our day faith healing is having quite a vogue, because of the extraordinary influence of such healers as Oral Roberts in

Healing in Modern Protestantism

America, and Harry Edwards in Britain. The former is a fundamentalist in theology and works within the tradition to which all fundamentalist faith healers belong; the latter is a spiritualistic healer who claims that his cures are effected by help of "spirit doctors" in the unseen world; and each of them is but an outstanding example of a fairly large company of faith healers of the class to which he belongs.

Oral Roberts is a minister of the Church known as the Assemblies of God. He is a man of vibrant and dominating personality, a fluent speaker with a flair for the dramatic, a shrewd master of assemblies, and good at spectacular showmanship. He has a remarkable grasp of practical psychology. Because of his showmanship and salesmanship—aided and abetted by such media of mass communication as the radio and television—he is probably the best-known faith healer in the English-speaking world. He has made good publicity use of the fact that strong opposition in Melbourne, Australia, led him to cut short his "Million Souls Crusade" in that country; and in all likelihood it has increased his popularity and influence in America.

The healing evangelist's huge tent congregations consist of people of all sorts and conditions, from little children to aged men and women. It seems to be a cross-section of American life, young and old, poor and well-to-do, illiterate and well-educated, the socially obscure and the socially prominent, the healthy and the sick—especially the sick. Most of his hearers are seeking something vital for their lives, though many of them might be hard put to say exactly what it is they are after. At its lowest, it is a craving for some emotional uplift that could bring a little color into otherwise drab lives. At its highest, it is the search for God, for that which alone can give meaning to a seemingly meaningless existence. Most

FAITH HEALING

of all there are thousands of sick people who are yearning for physical wholeness. Perhaps they have gone to doctor after doctor, to hospital after hospital, to nostrum after nostrum, but are none the better for all their striving and for all the money they have spent. Many of them perhaps have been given up by the medical profession. Now they are looking for a miracle—God's supernatural intervention through His human instrument, Oral Roberts. Obviously the evangelist is a man of immense power and is able to get his message across to most of the people who crowd his healing services.

He claims to have healed many people. Some of these healings are witnessed on television. It should be remembered, however, that what is seen on television is an edited film, portraying only the successes. Nor do we learn what happens afterwards to those who are claimed as cured. It would be interesting to know if there is any follow-up program to make sure that the cures really are cures. And if some cures are proved to be permanent, it would be of service to know (a) the proportion of permanent to temporary cures; (b) the proportion of the cures achieved in the healing line to the failures; and (c) the number of the alleged cures that are genuine cases of spiritual healing or that are only (and this is not to decry them) examples of mental or psychological healing, i.e., healing by hypnotic suggestion. There are bound to be failures. Oral Roberts is careful to point out that not every one who gets into the healing line is cured. But "hope springs eternal in the human breast," and Roberts maintains that his prayers go with these failures and that ultimately God, in His own good time, will heal all those who have true faith.

Harry Edwards is a layman, not an ordained minister. In his young manhood he was an agnostic and had no interest in spiritualism. One day, however, he attended a seance—in a skeptical frame of mind—and was convinced of the genuineness of the phenomena he witnessed. He joined a "development circle" and ere long came to the conclusion that he could heal under spirit control. Early successes strengthened his desire to exercise this ministry, and it is now his lifework.

He claims 6000 cures at least, but he disclaims that he himself possesses healing power. He is but the agent or instrument of discarnate spirit doctors who work through him. And any who desire to heal the sick, as the agents of these spirit doctors, can be successful healers if they will take the trouble to develop the two essential qualities of "simplicity" and "attunement with the heavenly host."

That this person has some cures to his credit cannot be disputed, and that they are the result of the power of hypnotic suggestion is a likely explanation. The theory that the cures are brought about by the activity of spirit doctors may not be true; but it is as hard to disprove as it is to prove. At any rate, the evidence for the reality of the many cures which he claims is quite flimsy, and is not likely to be acceptable to anyone of a scientific turn of mind.

A different type of healing ministry characterizes four people whose names, through their work and writings, have become quite familiar to a large circle of people—two of them doctors and two of them wives of ministers.

The late Dr. Rebecca Beard was an American woman physician who midway in her professional career became convinced of the reality of spiritual healing, and devoted the rest of her life to treating sick people by nonphysical means, relying almost entirely upon intercessory prayer. Both her philosophy of healing and her successes in curing even cases of organic diseases, including cancer, are set forth in a triology of books: *Everyman's Search, Everyman's Goal,* and *Everyman's Mission.*

FAITH HEALING

Dr. Christopher Woodard is a distinguished London physician who specializes in the treatment of soft-tissue injuries acquired in sports. He says that his experience with athletes made it easier for him to believe the importance of the mental factor in the treatment of *all* diseases. But when his two-year-old son was stricken with fulminating meningitis so seriously that he was near death's door, it was the prayers and faith of the parents, and of hundreds of friends, that restored him to health and strength. This experience brought Dr. Woodard to the unshakable conviction that spiritual healing is a reality. In his three books, *A Doctor Heals By Faith, A Doctor's Faith Holds Fast,* and *A Doctor's Faith Still Holds,* he gives moving testimony to the power of intercessory prayer in the treatment of every kind of disease, refusing to regard any sickness—even inoperable cancer—as beyond the healing power of the Great Physician. But it is prayer combined with other methods, both medical and extra-medical. Dr. Woodard's own words are worth quoting: "For myself I believe, as a doctor, that one should use in healing all the modern discoveries of medical science, but combine them with 'guidance.' It is impossible to generalize, but I find in my own personal experience that God uses all sorts of channels of healing; they may not fit into one's own picture of what is right and what is wrong according to medical etiquette."[8]

Mrs. Agnes Sanford is the China-born daughter of Southern Presbyterian missionaries and the wife of an American Episcopal clergyman. In her book *The Healing Light* she sets forth her conviction that God's creative and healing power can flow through anyone who will but open up his or her heart and mind to the Divine Spirit. The one essential qualification required in the person who would be a bearer of the healing light is complete surrender to God's mighty energy. Any other qualification is secondary.

Healing in Modern Protestantism

Mrs. Elsie H. Salmon is the wife of a Methodist minister in the Union of South Africa. Her four books, *He Heals Today, The Key to Healing, Christ Heals Again,* and *Christ Still Heals,* recount the amazing results flowing from twenty years of simple faith in the Healing Christ. It is an astonishing —almost unbelievable—record of the triumph of the spiritual principle in the conflict with human ailments and diseases; yet the story bears all the marks of genuineness.

All four of these spiritual healers—two within the medical tradition and two outside it—are convinced that our Lord's commission to His first disciples to "heal the sick" has never been withdrawn. They show—with actual and well-attested case histories from their own practices and ministries—that the Great Physician still puts forth His healing touch in the world today through the instrumentality of those who fully rely upon Him in faith and prayer.

5 Healing and the Prayer of Faith

SOME OF THE medieval mystics were accustomed to speak of the "ladder of prayer" stretching up from human need to God's power and willingness to satisfy that need. The lowest rung of the ladder is the cry for deliverance from some external physical danger; as, for example, in the case of shipwrecked mariners in the storm, or soldiers on the eve of battle. The highest rung of the ladder is the prayer of absolute surrender to the will of God, the greatest example being that of Christ in the Garden of Gethsemane praying, "O my Father, if it be possible, let this cup pass from me: nevertheless, not as I will, but as thou wilt." The prayer for the healing of sickness and affliction would probably be rated as being nearer to the bottom of the ladder than to the top by those who have never had much personal experience of illness. But there are many people who, believing that God's will is our health as well as our peace, would put this kind of prayer—especially when it is offered for others rather than for themselves—very near the highest rung of the prayer ladder. For they have come to believe that in this matter of healing "prayer moves the arm that moves the world" and that "more things are wrought by prayer than this world dreams of."

Healing and the Prayer of Faith

And they have actual case histories on their side—so many of them, indeed, that there seems to be more than enough evidence to affirm that spiritual healing is an established fact. Perhaps it does not take place as often as some easily persuaded people believe; on the other hand, it may happen more frequently than the more skeptical folk among us are prepared to admit. There are too many instances on record—cases which are clear-cut and about which there can be not the shadow of doubt—for us to be able reasonably to deny the fact of spiritual healing. That some professional faith healers exploit the possibilities of spiritual healing, and like to make exaggerated claims as to their own powers (even when they say, "It is not I who heals, but God"), should not induce us to close our eyes to the plain and honest testimony of many reliable witnesses.

Dr. Alexis Carrel, the famous medical scientist who wrote the best-seller, *Man the Unknown,* was convinced upon the basis of his own personal experience that miracles of healing are possible. He won the Nordhoff-Jung medal for cancer research, so he ought to have known a cancer when he saw one. He testified that he once saw a cancerous sore shrivel up into a scar before his very eyes, after earnest prayer. That, and other experiences, convinced him that prayer "is the most powerful form of energy we know," and he adds, "The influence of prayer on the human mind and body is as demonstrable as that of secreting glands. Its results can be measured in terms of increased physical buoyancy, greater intellectual vigor, moral stamina and a deeper understanding of the realities underlying human relationships."[1]

In the spring of 1937 Dr. Leslie D. Weatherhead, in an address to the British Methodist Conference, cited three cases of spiritual healing through prayer: (1) An airman, suffering in a hospital from an incurable disease, went back to work

FAITH HEALING

after prayers had been offered for him. (2) A woman, paralyzed in both legs, was able to walk again within two or three hours of being prayed for. (3) A blind woman, at 7:30 one Sunday night, found her sight restored. At that hour 2500 people were praying for her in the City Temple, London.

As is well known, Dr. Weatherhead has, over a quarter of a century, developed the concept of spiritual healing, both theoretically and practically. In his most recent book, *Psychology, Religion, and Healing,* he covers the whole subject from every angle. He relates several cases of spiritual healing, the most striking being that of a four-year-old boy suffering from nephritis. The mother, a nurse, had been a member of Dr. Weatherhead's congregation. After her marriage she went to live in North Wales, and it was there that her little son was taken seriously ill. The decided opinion of all the doctors who knew the case—including some well-known specialists—was that the boy was bound to die. The distracted mother wrote to her former minister, beseeching his help. Dr. Weatherhead brought the matter before his congregation, asking the people to join with him in praying for the little lad's healing. To the amazement of all the doctors, the boy made a complete recovery. "It is a miracle," was the general testimony, and the family doctor wrote to the mother, "You may tell Dr. Weatherhead that personally I am *quite sure* that prayer played the biggest part in your son's cure." Dr. Weatherhead adds a comment for those who might object that the little boy would have recovered even if no prayers had been offered on his behalf. Had the boy regained his health subsequent to his having taken some drug, no one would say that he would have recovered in any case; the cure would be ascribed to the drug, and the drug would soon be in universal use. The implication is obvious.[2]

The name of Dr. Howard Somervell is well known to many.

Healing and the Prayer of Faith

He is a Fellow of the Royal College of Surgeons, London. He was a member of the Mount Everest expedition which, in 1922, climbed nearly to the top of the highest mountain in the world. In his book, *After Everest,* Dr. Somervell tells of an Indian schoolmaster with a tubercular disease that had reached the well-nigh incurable stage. It was decided on high medical authority that the only way to save the man was by amputating a leg. When the man was told of the doctors' decision, he said, "Will you give me three weeks? I want to see what effect constant praying will have." The doctors reluctantly gave their consent, and the man was discharged from the hospital. He went home. Three weeks later he was back at the hospital, showing marked signs of improvement. A chain of prayer was kept up by his family and friends. The man's improvement continued. In a few months he was completely healed, back at school, teaching his classes, playing games with the boys, running about on both legs without the slightest sign of disease or disability.

Dr. Somervell relates another case of miraculous healing through prayer. His patient was suffering from cancer of the cheek, and it was so advanced as to be inoperable. The man left the hospital and went home to die. There was only one thing left to do and that was to pray. He went to his church and asked the members to pray for him. They did, and in a very short time the cancer was nothing more than a healed scar. Says Dr. Somervell, "The cancer, incurable by any method known to medical science, except radium and X-rays, had completely disappeared. I confess that in my weakness of faith I was amazed, but of the original diagnosis there can be no doubt. If we in Neyyoor, where we see five or six hundred cases of cancer of the mouth every year, cannot diagnose a case of it, who can? Explain these cases how you like, by the power of mind over body, or by the intervention of God—the fact remains that their faith had been exercised in a way of which in our materialistic England we have no experience."[3]

Dr. Sherwood Eddy, a highly respected figure in the religious world, was a levelheaded man, with a sound educational background, and a wide experience in many countries, in work among college students and in Y.M.C.A. service. In his book *You Will Survive After Death* a number of cases of spiritual healing, some of them the most remarkable on record, are reported from firsthand knowledge. Here is one of them. There lived in London a man by the name of W. T. Parrish. His wife was dying of cancer, and had undergone one almost fatal operation. She had reached a stage where she was beyond the help of medical science. She urged her distracted husband that they try spiritual healing. At first, he was much opposed to the idea. He himself was a man of fine physique, an instructor in fencing, boxing, and physical culture generally; and he was not averse to saying that spiritual healing and the like were only for weak-minded women and naïve men. But, driven by the desperate necessity of his wife's seemingly hopeless condition, he began to feel that there might be something in what she said. He commenced to pray for her recovery, and increasingly came to believe that he would be used of God in the healing of his wife. After nine months of intense and earnest prayer Mrs. Parrish was completely cured, and no further operations were necessary. From then onward until his death Mr. Parrish devoted his life to spiritual healing, and there is evidence that he healed many people and helped many more. "He believed that a tide of spiritual life flowed through him in this ministry, that these were among the 'greater works' promised by Christ, and that the church should never have

Healing and the Prayer of Faith

lost this ministry of healing so prevalent and effective with Christ Himself and in the early Christians."[4]

Dr. John Heuss is the rector of Trinity Episcopal Church, New York City. In a recent volume of sermons entitled *Our Christian Vocation* he records two striking cases of spiritual healing. Here is the more remarkable of the two. One of his parishioners, an elderly woman, broke her leg three times in rapid succession. She was confined to bed for a number of years. Much additional tragedy came her way, and she lost all power to pray and all belief in the efficacy of prayer. One day Dr. Heuss talked to her about healing miracles, including those associated with Lourdes. She said that she wished she could exercise enough faith to be cured, but feared that she was beyond it. A little later the rector called on the woman again, and to his surprise found her out of bed and walking around the house. This is what she told him. After his previous visit she decided to throw the whole burden of her affliction upon God in earnest, believing prayer. She prayed and prayed and prayed, until exhausted she fell asleep. In the midst of her sleep she heard a voice say, "Arise, you are able to walk." She got up there and then, completely healed. And Dr. Heuss adds, "Since that day I have never doubted that God can and does perform miracles of healing."

Such cases as these can be multiplied from the literature of spiritual healing—and there is an abundance of such literature —but it will suffice here to record but one more. It is the remarkable story of Iris, from the casebook of Mrs. Salmon. She was to have her left leg amputated in three days. Thirteen months before, an operation on the hip had brought about complete paralysis of the leg, which had become withered and had doubled up. What Iris regarded as Divine guidance induced her to seek the help of Mrs. Salmon, some miles

FAITH HEALING

away, which involved a train journey. After hearing the girl's story and getting from her the assurance that she was certain the Great Physician would heal her, Mrs. Salmon prayed with her, asking Christ to restore the leg to perfect health. "I made sweeping strokes down her spine and then took the withered, bent and paralyzed limb in my hands.... Then I said, 'Christ, my Master, do Your work,' and with these words the leg immediately straightened out before our eyes and this dead limb at once became filled with life." So wrote Mrs. Salmon. After giving thanks for the miracle, Iris put on a brand new shoe she had brought with her—so strong was her faith—and walked to the railway station, refusing the offer of a drive. When she arrived home, her mother, seeing her walking normally and without crutches (she had left them as mementos with Mrs. Salmon), was so amazed that she fainted. Iris had promised the healer that she would report to the doctors. She did so at a time when they were discussing the proposed amputation. They, too, were amazed when they saw her standing before them perfectly healed, and asked to examine the "dead" leg. They were further amazed to discover that the withered flesh had become perfectly healthy, and that the temperature of the once "dead" leg was now normal. Iris says, "I know that it was God who healed me. But He not only healed my leg. He gave me Faith that nothing can destroy."[5]

Even a casual examination of the above cases, as they have been reported, reveals two striking facts. One is that some of them, at least—and it may be all of them—are clearly examples of the healing of *organic* diseases. The other is that in all of them the *prayer of faith* played—or seems to have played—a central part in bringing about the cure.

The first fact is attested to by two distinguished medical men, Dr. Alexis Carrel and Dr. Howard Somervell. Surely,

Healing and the Prayer of Faith

with their scientific training and with no professional ax to grind, they were capable of making a truly objective judgment! Between them they put their *imprimatur* on two cases of cancer cure and one case of the healing of a tubercular leg. And in the other recorded cases there seems to be medical attestation in the background; as in the letter sent by the family doctor to the mother of the boy who had nearly died of nephritis. But even if such background testimony were not forthcoming, there is no reason to suspect the honest reporting of Dr. Leslie D. Weatherhead, Dr. Sherwood Eddy, Dr. John Heuss, and Mrs. Elsie Salmon, or to question the soundness of their interpretation.

The fact that organic diseases yield to spiritual and psychological factors most assuredly disposes of the contention that spiritual healing is confined wholly to *functional* disorders. There are many people who believe that purely functional disorders—disorders in which injury to bodily structure or brain tissue is entirely absent—may respond to the operations of the suggestion-mechanism evoked by modern psychiatry and psychotherapy. But diseases in which organic lesions are involved, in which there are changes in physical structure or damage to a specific organ, these, they maintain, are beyond the healing power of mind or spirit, even of the Divine Spirit. No cure of physical affliction is possible except by physical means, and when such physical healings by nonphysical techniques are claimed by enthusiastic faith healers then they must have misread the facts of the case—or so it is said.

Of course, the distinction between organic and functional disorders is convenient. But it must not be pressed too far. It may be illustrated thus. There was a popular evangelist in the last generation, named John MacNeil. He drew great crowds wherever he went. He was a very outspoken preacher, and

FAITH HEALING

often gave great offense to some hearers by his caustic comments. He was holding a series of services in an English city, and one of his regular hearers was an old gentleman who had been paralyzed for years. He was brought to the meeting in a wheel chair, and because he was somewhat deaf was wheeled down to a place near the preacher just under the pulpit. One night John MacNeil, in his sermon, made some strong remarks which a man sitting up in the balcony of the church resented. The man jumped to his feet and shouted "Liar!" But the helpless old gentleman mistook the cry for "Fire!" and to the surprise of all around him—and perhaps most of all to himself— he lifted himself out of his wheel chair and reached the exit on his legs in quite a short time. It is obvious that he had been suffering from "hysterical paralysis," which is a functional, not an organic, disorder. But supposing he had injured his spinal cord in, say, an automobile accident, and that the nerve-fibers and tissue had not regenerated; in that case his paralysis would have been the result of this organic lesion, and had the building been really on fire, he could not have escaped unless he were carried or wheeled out.

The differentiation of the two types of illness is useful as far as it goes. Prof. L. W. Grensted remarks that "the distinction between functional and organic, however useful, is so obscure that it creates difficulties at every turn."[6] This is probably an exaggeration. But it is necessary to be warned against making the distinction a hard and fast one. "Body" and "mind" belong to two different worlds—the material and the immaterial. The one can be weighed and measured, the other cannot be; the one has location in space, the other has not; the one can be touched and handled, the other is beyond physical contact. A leg can be amputated, but not a thought; a stomach ulcer can be X-rayed, but not an anxiety neurosis. And yet "body" and

Healing and the Prayer of Faith

"mind" are a unity, in which the material and the immaterial constantly interact. The ancient Greek philosopher, Aristotle, observed that "the soul is the essence of the whole living body." He knew that "body" and "mind" influence each other, but although we today know more about these two entities than he did, the way in which they actually interact is as puzzling to us as it was to him. Indeed, we have not got beyond the view expressed by Thomas H. Huxley, the famous nineteenth-century scientist, to the effect that the "nexus" between "matter" and "spirit" is unthinkable.

But that there *is* a connection cannot be doubted. Philosophers and psychologists may theorize about it; we ordinary people know it from everyday experience. News is brought to you of the death of a loved one, and your heart beats faster, your pulse goes quicker, your face blanches, and you may even tremble and faint. The message "John is dead," which, of course, is a thought in the mind, immediately produces bodily effects. Or you may have a persistent pain in your chest, which gets worse as the days go by, despite all you do to get rid of it; and you begin to worry lest it indicate some really serious condition. The worry is a state of mind induced by a bodily state. A dream—which is mental—may be the outcome of a heavy meal late at night—which is physical. But the dream may cause the dreamer to awaken with a sudden start—a mental state giving rise to a physical one. And this interaction of body and mind goes on, more or less, every waking moment, and it may be every sleeping moment as well.

It is common knowledge nowadays that a sick mind can bring about a sick body; a good illustration is the familiar one of stomach ulcers forming as the result of excessive worry. It is also common knowledge that the opposite is true, that a sick body can create a sick mind, as, for example, in the case of the man who commits suicide through mental depression brought about by the conviction that he has an incurable disease. Martin Luther remarked: "Heavy thoughts bring on physical maladies; when the soul is oppressed, so is the body." But we may turn this statement around and say, "Physical maladies bring on heavy thoughts; when the body is oppressed, so is the soul."

If it be true that the mind can influence the body in the direction of ill health (and likewise the body influence the mind in the same direction) then it must be false to say that bodily ills are beyond the reach of the forces of mind and spirit. Competent medical authority has stated that no physical tissue is wholly removed from the impact of powers that are nonphysical. The previously quoted testimony from the *British Medical Journal* can be supported in other influential quarters. William McDougall was an expert in both biology and physiology, though he gained his international reputation as a psychologist. In his monumental work, *Body and Mind,* he wrote: "Successful therapeutic suggestions and actions that effect definite tissue changes are especially significant in the present connection; for in all such cases we have definite evidence of control of bodily processes which, though unconsciously effected, must be regarded as physical. Of the limits of this power of mental control over the organic processes of the body we are altogether ignorant, and new evidence . . . repeatedly warns us against setting up any arbitrary limit to what may be effected in this way."[7] Prof. Karl Heim, the famous theologian-scientist, quotes from a German medical authority this significant statement: "Liek, who is a doctor, ventures to write this far-reaching sentence. 'There is no functional disturbance in the living body, no illness, whether we call it functional or organic, which is not amenable in a greater or less degree to influence

Healing and the Prayer of Faith

brought to bear on the soul. This, to take a most grim example, is true even of cancer.'"[8] On the same page, Prof. Heim adds his own weighty opinion: "In principle, therefore, no limits whatever are set here to the spiritual influencing from within of the process of illness. This fact has a liberating effect, especially when one considers the paralyzing effect on the soul of an invalid of the thought, characteristic of the age of causal mechanism that the infirmity must take its course through his body with the unalterable necessity of a machine and that he is caught and mangled in its merciless wheels . . . now we are able to break free from the overwhelming power of this causal-mechanical picture of nature which works on suffering people like a 'bad suggestion' and hinders them from bringing their spiritual power into action against the disease."

Many doctors—it may be the medical profession as a whole—are not prepared to believe this. They are still the prisoners of nineteenth-century medicine, the point of view of which was predominantly materialistic. Only physical methods can cure physical ills—so it was believed then, and the tradition still holds sway, though unconscious sway, in many medical minds today. When confronted with the psychological or spiritual cure of some organic malady, they explain it by saying that it is a case of wrong diagnosis in the first place or it is the result of "spontaneous remission" of the disease. These are the reasons given in the report on faith healing recently issued by the British Medical Association. That august body would not deny that nonphysical methods can cure nonphysical afflictions, but it is not prepared to say that organic lesions can be healed by other than medicine and surgery.

Of course, it has to be admitted some organic disturbances—cancer, for example—sometimes seem to cure themselves, without any help from physician or surgeon. But it is claimed to be a very rare occurrence. Some authorities say that the cases of the "spontaneous regression" of cancer is about one in 14,000; others say one in about 100,000. But they are both only guesses. Two medical researchers, Drs. Warren H. Cole and Tilden C. Everson, have been making a survey of the problem on behalf of the American Cancer Society.[9] They have found it hard to obtain trustworthy information, but think that there are a few cases of "spontaneous regression." A previous large-scale study of this problem was undertaken in 1918, and covered the period 1890-1916. The report listed 302 cases, an average of about eleven a year. Drs. Cole and Everson reject all but eighty-eight of these on the grounds of insufficient evidence, and think that another twenty or thirty may have to be thrown out after further examination.

How many of these people had come into contact with some form of psychological or spiritual healing we have no means of telling, but we do know that—apart from the relatively small number of cases reported by the medical profession—many such cases of so-called "spontaneous regression" occur in faith healing circles. Nor, when they do occur, must they always be placed in the category of "mistaken diagnosis." To regard them as such may seem to be in obedience to the scientific demand for accuracy, but is it really so? May it not rather be an expression of ingrained conservatism (often a very good thing), or even the inveterate prejudice (never a good thing), of the medical profession?

We may admit that there must be many cases of "mistaken diagnosis" in the realm of faith healing cures (but they *are* cures of *some* malady, nonetheless), but there must be many more that cannot be so characterized. If they are *all* to be put in this class, then it is high time the medical profession took steps to reduce their number, either by improving diagnostic

Healing and the Prayer of Faith

techniques or by putting an embargo on incompetents. But faith cures cannot all be explained in this snap manner. Cases of proved cancer and tuberculosis—proved, that is, by medical tests—have been healed after prayer, as the testimony of such men as Dr. Alexis Carrel and Dr. Howard Somervell amply demonstrates. To which may be added the case of a girl reported in Dr. Edwin Ash's *Faith and Suggestion*. The girl was stated by her medical attendant—"a practitioner of many years' experience and high qualifications"—to be suffering, on definite evidence, from tuberculosis in a very advanced stage. She was, almost instantly, completely and definitely cured by "faith."[10]

Surely the question can be raised: Why is it that so many of these cases of so-called "natural remission," or "spontaneous regression," take place in faith healing circles? And why so few in orthodox medical practice? Might it not be, after all, that the prayer of faith *does* have something to do with the healing of the sick, even the organically sick? Might it not further be that this prayer of faith releases a divine energy that cannot be explained in purely medical or surgical terms?

And if it may be argued that there are cases of "natural remission" in which no prayers have been offered, one may ask, How do you know this? The sick person may not pray for himself (though that can be doubted, for it seems likely that most afflicted people will secretly pray in their innermost minds), and he may not hear anyone's prayer for his recovery, but it does not necessarily follow that his is a prayerless case. Very few men and women are so bereft of friends as to have no one, in their time of desperate need, to remember them in prayer.

But even if only functional disturbances were cured by faith healing, a long list of healings would have to be chalked up.

FAITH HEALING

Even cases which psychiatrists have found to be intractable have yielded to the prayer of faith. Dr. Weatherhead tells of one such case from his own experience. It concerned a seventeen-year-old girl from the country, whose psychological troubles manifested themselves in the queerest physical symptoms. Feeling that she needed more help than he could give, he referred her to a well-known London psychiatrist. The doctor spent much time with the girl, but made no impression whatsoever; and so he sent her back home, saying nothing further could be done. Months later Dr. Weatherhead came to the conclusion that the case had been too easily given up. So he wrote to the girl's mother to tell her and her daughter that on the next Sunday evening the City Temple congregation would pray for the girl. There was an immediate good response. The girl improved at once, and has remained well ever since.[11]

The evidence is clear. The prayer of faith works. It seems that in the struggle between sickness and health true prayer tips the balance in favor of recovery. The noted British psychologist, Dr. James A. Hadfield, bears testimony to this truth. "I am convinced that the Christian religion is one of the most valuable and potent influences that we possess for producing that harmony and peace of mind and that confidence of soul which are needed to bring health and power to a large proportion of nervous patients. In some cases I have attempted to cure nervous patients with suggestions of quietness and confidence, but without success until I have linked these suggestions to that faith in the power of God which is the substance of the Christian's confidence and hope."[12]

How does the prayer of faith work? How does it manage to tip the balance in favor of recovery from sickness? We do not know. But that is no argument against its reality and validity. It is said by the medical profession that aspirin is the most

Healing and the Prayer of Faith

effective analgesic for ordinary use, but no doctor can say how it manages to kill pain. But we know that it does, and that is sufficient. We may not understand how the prayer of faith "availeth much" in the healing of men's sicknesses, but that it does is beyond all dispute.

6 Healing and the Reign of Law

THE GREATEST MIRACLE in the universe is the universe itself. It is full of wonderful things, but none is more wonderful than its own existence, unless it be that part of creation that can wonder at the whole of it, man himself. Traditional Christian theology has always been ready to assert this, but no thinker of the past has done it more pointedly and emphatically than the great Church Father of the fourth century, St. Augustine. All the miraculous things that take place in nature, so he says, are not so miraculous as the universe itself, our world and the heavens and all contained therein; and all the wonderful things that man by his knowledge and ingenuity can achieve are not so great a miracle as is man himself.

Nor would the modern philosopher and scientist disagree with this. Man's attempt to understand the universe, in his philosophical speculations and scientific constructions, began in a feeling of wonder, as both Plato and Aristotle said long ago; and that feeling of wonder has increased, not decreased, the more men have discovered about the natural and spiritual order of which they form a part. The achievements of this electronic and atomic age would overwhelm with amazement the primitive savage—indeed, even the civilized European and

Healing and the Reign of Law

American of half a century ago—but they are still more wonderful to the men who made them possible, the contemporary mathematician, physicist, and engineer. New discoveries and new achievements do not drive out of the universe the miraculous (in the sense in which we are using the term here); rather they increase our sense of mystery and deepen our feeling of wonder.

As for man, he is still "Man the Unknown," the ultimate mystery within the universe; and of all created beings he is the one alone for whom the mystery exists. The "electronic brain" —the so-called "thinking machine"—is a most wonderful and complicated contraption of wires and tubes. It can solve the most complex problems, make the most complicated computations, within a few minutes, whereas it would take a small army of experts months to achieve the same results. Yet the machine does not really think, or even if it does (something we can affirm only by stretching the meaning of the term "think"), it does not know that it thinks. It is not conscious. Certainly it is not *self*-conscious. It does not know what it is doing, nor can it take pleasure in what it achieves. The human mind transcends the electronic brain, for without the former the latter would not exist. Man the thinker—man the inventor—has to conceive and plan, design and construct the wonderful machine. It did not, because it could not, produce itself. Man himself is therefore a greater miracle than even the most miraculous children of his own knowledge and skill.

The supreme miracle of the universe is the miracle of law and order that makes the universe what it is. This supreme miracle is the expression of the twofold fundamental principle of the Unity and Uniformity of Nature. The name by which we call it implies this. *Uni*-verse means *one* verse, *one* song, *one* system. All existing things, from the most minute speck of

FAITH HEALING

dust on the earth's surface to the most distant galaxy of heavenly bodies, are bound together in one unimaginable vastness. Even if it is true—as modern astronomy assures us—that we live in an ever-expanding universe, and even if for the sake of convenience we may speak of universes within the universe, it does not alter the fact that it is both logically and physically (or should we say "electrically"?) one system. As one of our philosophers illustrates it, a red-haired fisherman gets up at six o'clock one morning and goes fishing; he catches three large trout. If we could go back far enough, probably to infinity (which, of course, is impossible), we would find some sort of connection between the color of the fisherman's hair and the number and size of the fish he caught on that particular morning. True, the illustration seems farfetched, but if the order of nature is a logically and physically connected system, then everything that happens is inevitably and irrevocably wrapped up in "the bundle of life."

The truth that the universe is really a *uni*-verse is expressed by scientists and philosophers in various ways. In addition to speaking of the unity and uniformity of Nature, they also talk of the Law of Sufficient Reason, the Law of Universal Causation, and the principle of the conservation of energy. The Law of Sufficient Reason means that there must be a reason for everything that happens, for even the slightest change that takes place in the order of events; and this must be so even if no one knows the reason. The Law of Universal Causation means that for every event there must be a cause adequate to produce it, that cause and effect are indissolubly connected; and this, after all, is only a restatement of the Law of Sufficient Reason. And the principle of the conservation of energy is the doctrine that the amount of energy in the universe is constant, that it never increases nor decreases. It cannot be destroyed, not

Healing and the Reign of Law

even the smallest quantity of it; though it may change its form, as when a certain amount of electricity is transformed into a certain amount of heat, or light, or chemical action. The mode is different, but the quantity is the same. Thus the total quantity of actual and potential energy in the universe is, according to this doctrine, a constant.

But it is just because of this miracle of the universe, this miracle of law and order—the "reign of law," as it is commonly called—that so many people today deny the possibility of any other kind of miracle. To speak of the miracle of the universe is just a way of acknowledging the wondrous splendor and logical coherence of the totality of things. But when we speak of miracles in the usual sense we are thinking of alleged breaches of the reign of law, of events that seemingly break up the sequence of cause and effect, of happenings that are apparent intrusions into nature's orderly processes. Such miracles, we are told, cannot happen. No modern writer has stated this point more incisively and dogmatically than the eighteenth-century skeptical Scottish philosopher, David Hume. "A miracle," he writes, "is a violation of the laws of nature; and as a firm and unalterable experience has established these laws, the proof against a miracle, from the very nature of the fact, is as entire as any argument from experience can possibly be imagined."[1]

Of course, the meaning of "miracle" is relative both to the level of creaturely existence and to the level of human understanding. What on one level of existence might be regarded as a "miracle" would on a higher level be accepted as a perfectly natural happening. For a rosebush to pull itself up by the roots and walk round the garden would be a "miracle," but for a sleeping dog to bestir itself and chase a cat over the fence is in the "order of nature." For a dog to get up on its hind legs

FAITH HEALING

and make a speech to the local medical association would be miraculous, but for a man to stand up before an audience and give an address would be a most natural procedure. We can push the illustration further and apply it to our Lord. For an ordinary human being to quiet a raging tempest by a simple command, or to multiply a few loaves and fishes to feed a great company of people, or to restore to life a young man on his way to burial, would be a "miracle" of the first order, but to one who belongs to a higher sphere of reality it could be the natural thing to do. Christ belonged to that higher order of reality. To those who move on a lower level of existence His "mighty works" are miraculous in character. But for Him to perform them was quite natural.

Miracles are also relative to the level of human understanding. Events and devices which to us today are quite understandable, a savage would inevitably regard as manifestations of supernatural power, and would undoubtedly be terrified thereby. Some years ago a missionary in Central Africa was threatened by a group of hostile natives. He was in a situation from which he could not retreat, and things looked ominous. Then his wits came to the rescue (or was it an inspiration from heaven?); he took out his artificial teeth, upper and lower dentures, and making a biting movement with them in his hand, turned them towards the tribesmen. They were terror-stricken, and in a few moments had all vanished into the bush. For a man to be able to remove his teeth from his mouth was to them a miracle. It was surely against their idea of "nature."

There are very many things in this wonderful age in which we live that to the people of the last century would have seemed impossible. Long ago there were soothsayers of the type of "Mother Shipton" and "Nostradamus" who were supposed to have foretold some of the wonders of the future, such

Healing and the Reign of Law

as that carriages would run without horses and that men would be ably to fly through the air like birds. It is certain that they were not believed in their day and age. "Carriages run without horses!" "Men fly through the air like birds!" They are miracles and that kind of miracle cannot happen. Yet they do happen although they have no real relationship to the old-time predictions. Had our nineteenth-century forbears—who lived in what they regarded as pre-eminently the age of science—been told that men would speed through the air three times faster than the speed of sound, that people would sit in their own homes and by turning a button or pressing a switch be able to listen to music or look at an event originating hundreds of miles away, that scientists would be able to solve problems of atomic fission and fusion, that nations would be able to manufacture explosives of such terrific force that one small bomb could destroy a whole city—had they been told of these and of other things, like the telephone and the X-ray machine, they would have laughed derisively, and exclaimed: "Why, those are miracles, and such miracles do not happen! Such things are against nature and will never come to pass!" But such things have come to pass. To us they are not miracles in the sense that they are contrary to the laws of nature, for we can understand them (at least, the experts can); though they are miracles in the sense that they increase our feelings of amazement at the wondrous things twentieth-century man is able to do through his understanding and control of facts and forces of nature.

"With God all things are possible," said Christ. He surely meant all things that do not contradict the Divine Nature, for the Supreme Being cannot be untrue to Himself. But it is equally true to assert that there are no miracles to God. This must be the case if what we finite creatures call "miracles" are

FAITH HEALING

relative to knowledge and to level of existence. God is the Eternal Reality. He is not one being among many; He is the One Being on whom everything else depends. Since He is omniscient, His knowledge is complete; and since He is omnipresent, no part of the universe is bereft of His presence. No law of nature is outside His ken. There is no event of which He is not cognizant, no place where He is not. The whole vast intricate complexity of cause-effect is within His control, and He cannot be taken by surprise. There are no gaps in His knowledge; all possibilities and potentialities are open to His gaze. In this sense God cannot work miracles.

Nevertheless, to us humans—belonging to the finite order of existence and with our understanding of the universe far from complete—God's direction and control of the world must contain elements of the miraculous. There are points and times at which He seems to interfere with the natural order of events. That does not mean that His relationship to the world is that of a watchmaker to a watch, who although he made a very fine watch at the beginning is obliged to intervene to regulate it from time to time to make up for its imperfections. God is not identical with the universe. As Christian theology insists, He is transcendent; that is, He is over and above the natural order—as St. Paul says, "God over all, blessed for evermore." But He is not outside the universe. To put it in the language of theology, He is immanent in the world-process. He is not—as someone has vividly put it—a kind of almighty engineer who constructed this mighty engine of the universe, then pulled the throttle wide open, and jumped from the footplate, leaving the tremendous machine to rush along under its own power forever on the twin rails of natural law. God is the indwelling Spirit of the universe, sustaining its existence every moment by His almighty will, and guiding and controlling all

Healing and the Reign of Law

its operations. He is—as the Bible insists—the Life of the world, upholding all things by the word of His power.

This means, of course, that the Living God is Personal Reality. If He is immanent in the universe, then the world-process must itself be the sphere and medium of His personal action, and the order of nature must bear constant witness to the ever-present working of supernatural power. Thus the world-process is both natural and supernatural; or rather, the natural and the supernatural are but two aspects of the same fundamental reality. Hence, what we call "miracles" are not interferences with the scheme of things from the outside; they are within the natural order, and are not miracles to the transcendent-immanent God, but only to us with our limited powers and finite intelligence.

C. S. Lewis defines "miracle" as "an interference with Nature by supernatural power."[2] If it is "interference"—and the word is misleading in this connection—then it must not be taken to mean an arbitrary and lawless intrusion into the order of nature, and therefore contrary to it. If the world-process is the organ of God's personal activity, then Dr. H. E. Fosdick's definition is much more acceptable: "A miracle is God's use of His own law-abiding powers to work out in ways surprising to us His will for our lives and for the world." And he adds, as a personal testimony: "Unless the whole Christian Gospel is false, miracles in that sense are happening all the time. If I had not experienced them and seen them I should not be a Christian at all."[3] Such miraculous events cannot be opposed to the natural order, but only to our limited understanding of it. As St. Augustine put it: "We do not say that God does something contrary to nature because He acts in a way that is contrary to our knowledge of nature." Canon Alan Richardson, who quotes this saying of the great Church Father, observes: "Thus,

FAITH HEALING

a gramophone is a terrifying miracle from the standpoint of a savage; the cure of certain maladies by means of mental or spiritual agencies is still a miracle from ours. There is much in nature which in view of our limited knowledge in the field of empirical science must be deemed miraculous; from the standpoint of science certain things are miraculous today which may not appear miraculous to the scientists of tomorrow. The workings of the homing instincts of bees and pigeons, for example, will cease to be sheer miracle to us when scientists can give us a full account of them."[4]

No one sets forth this point of view better than that great Christian scholar and churchman, the late Archbishop William Temple. Speaking of the universe as the medium of the Eternal Spirit's never-ceasing personal action, he says it follows that "no Law of Nature as discovered by physical science is ultimate. It is a general statement of that course of conduct in nature which is sustained by the purposive action of God so long and so far as it will serve His purpose. No doubt it is true that the same cause will always produce the same effect in the same circumstances. Our contention is that an element in every actual cause, and indeed the determinate element, is the active purpose of God fulfilling itself with that perfect constancy which calls for an infinite graduation of adjustments in the process. Where any adjustment is so considerable as to attract notice it is called a miracle; but it is not a specimen of a special class, it is an illustration of the general character of the World-Process."[5]

In the *Yale Lectures on Preaching,* Dr. Henry Van Dyke expresses the same truth from a somewhat different angle— that of our Lord's thought about miracles. "Jesus did not think of God as having exhausted all possible modes of His activity in those which are familiar to us. His presence in the world is

Healing and the Reign of Law

of such a personal kind that it necessarily brings with it the power of direct, personal, infinitely varied action. Out of this power spring those strange signs and wondrous works which we call miracles. Jesus never said they were against nature."[6]

Why does the subject of faith healing and spiritual healing fit into this discussion? Simply because in the present limited state of our knowledge, the cure of men's maladies by such techniques as intercessory prayer must appear miraculous. There are many physical remedies which have beneficial results, but the doctors cannot explain just how they bring about physiological and chemical changes in the body (aspirin, for example, as indicated previously). That is why such remedies are known as "empirical." We know little about how the procedures of psychotherapy work to cure mental illness; and we know nothing at all of the way in which the prayer of faith operates in the healing of functional disorders, much less of organic diseases. But there are certain things of which we can be sure.

One is that cures *are* effected by physical, psychological, and spiritual techniques, and by a combination of any two or all three of them, despite the fact that there are many failures. Our knowledge is far from complete in these realms, our methods far from perfect, for success to be chalked up every time a sick person is treated. No doubt, the highest *percentage* of successes is to be found in the sphere of orthodox medicine and surgery, but psychiatrists and psychotherapists and spiritual healers have their victories also—victories that cannot reasonably be disputed.

We can be sure, too, that in every kind of healing, whatever the methods used, God is at work. Every cure is a manifestation of the power of God in action. And not a God who is far off in the some distant heaven, but the God who is within us.

FAITH HEALING

It is in Him, as St. Paul says, that "we live, and move, and have our being." Or, as Lord Tennyson puts it, in his poem, "The Higher Pantheism":

> Speak thou to Him, for He heareth,
> And spirit with spirit can meet;
> Closer is He than breathing,
> And nearer than hands or feet.

This applies to every realm of the healing art. Ambroise Paré, the great French doctor, used to say to his students: "Gentlemen, I bound the patient's wounds, God healed him." Today, the psychiatrist can say, "I analyzed the patient, God healed him." The psychotherapist can say, "I treated the patient, God healed him." And likewise, the spiritual healer can say, "I prayed for the patient, I laid my hands upon him, and God healed him."

We may also be sure that when God heals in response to the prayer of faith He no more contravenes the laws of nature than when a cure follows the administering of the so-called "miracle drugs" or the performance of a surgical operation. We have been taught to think of the universe as being governed by "natural law." Would it not be nearer the truth to say that the universe is governed *by God* according to natural law? After all, these laws are only man's way of saying that as far as he has been able to observe, certain events happen with unfailing regularity. But he cannot observe everything; he cannot trace the ramifications of every event; he does not know everything about the universe and its direction and control. How then can he be reasonably sure that nature has no exceptions, that no surprises can occur? Even the scientists warn us against being too cocksure in this matter. Contemporary physicists are not so enthusiastic about the principle of the con-

Healing and the Reign of Law

servation of energy. Some of them—Sir Arthur S. Eddington and Sir James Jeans—maintain that the laws of nature are not immutable, affirming that they are only "statistical averages." They even argue that there is a certain "freedom of the will" in the atoms. In view of this we dare not stubbornly persist in the belief that miracles are impossible.

Not if we believe in a Personal God who is immanent in the universe. God's ways are past finding out—at least, many of them. His wisdom is unsearchable. When we reflect upon the ways of God with man and with nature we cannot know what is possible or impossible, save that we can be sure that nothing He does can contradict His nature or be inconsistent with His purpose. Man can by his skill and knowledge alter the course of events to serve his purpose. Is the "Creator of the ends of the earth" less than that which He has made? Man can work within the framework of nature to bring about desired ends. Is his Maker less able to do the same? A page from personal experience can illustrate this.

When our son was a child he was playing on a swing and fell out on to the hard floor. There was a thud and a yell and a wail which brought his parents running to his help. Fortunately, beyond a bump on his forehead, he was not hurt. We did not leave him lying on the ground, although the law of gravitation—which had brought him to the ground—decreed that he should stay there. No, we picked him up and brushed away his tears. Did we breach the law of gravitation in so doing? Of course not. Yet in that instance, and in a sense, we "suspended" it, by calling in a higher law—the law of personal will. Had he been badly hurt other laws would have been utilized to convey him to the hospital, where still other laws would have been utilized by the doctors to combat his injuries. In all this, no law of nature would be broken. Rather, the understanding of some of these laws would be utilized to achieve a desired personal end—the healing of an injured lad. Is the infinite Father less able to desire and accomplish such an end—and without breaking any laws, too?

Here is a modern parable that may help us see this point more clearly.[7] Two children, a boy and a girl, were crossing the Atlantic in an ocean liner, the captain of which, being a relative, showed them much kindness. They had never been on a ship before, and naturally the great engines attracted much of their attention. They would stand and look down into the engine room, watching the smooth, regular movements of the colossal thing that propelled the ship. How it did this they were too young to understand, but they were old enough to perceive that there was a fixed order and regularity of movement. How the whole thing had been set in motion they did not know, for they had seen it only in action. Whenever they saw it, it was always moving; and some of the sailors told them that it kept on moving all through the night, even when the passengers were sleeping.

Now sometimes these two children would discuss whether or not this engine could be stopped, and whether the captain had any power over its movements. The little girl, who had great faith in the captain, was sure that he could stop it whenever he pleased. She argued that the engine must have been set going when the ship started, and that it would have to be stopped at the end of the voyage; and if so, then the captain could stop the engine any time he wished. Besides, some of the sailors told her that he sometimes did so in the course of a voyage.

The boy, on the other hand, was not so sure of this. He did not know how the engine had been set going, and perhaps the captain had nothing to do with it. All that he knew was that the machinery had always been moving when they saw it. How did they know what would happen at the close of the journey? Perhaps the ship might be stopped and the engines kept going. Or perhaps the engine might wear itself out. Or, if the great fires had anything to do with it, the captain might give orders for the fires to be put out when the ship was nearing the journey's end. But that at any moment, and in the middle of the voyage while the fires were still burning and the great machines were still going, the captain could suddenly stop the ship —well, that was too difficult to believe. Besides, even if he were able to do so, it did not follow that he had ever done so. True, some of the crew members said that they had seen him do this; but perhaps they were mistaken, or were telling tall stories. Thus the children argued in their own childish way.

One day the boy was playing on deck with a large, brightly-colored ball, when suddenly it bounced over the side of the ship into the sea. He was in great trouble over his loss and ran to tell his sister about it. He found her talking to the captain. "Oh," pleaded the girl, "do stop the ship and get the ball." But the captain smilingly replied, "What! Stop the ship's engines for that! Little boys should be more careful when playing ball." He spoke so kindly that the girl did not lose faith in her friend. But the boy was now quite certain that the captain could not stop the engines in mid-ocean, whatever a few sailors might say.

Later on in the day the children were allowed on the bridge where the captain was standing. Suddenly they heard a cry, "Man overboard!" In a moment they saw the captain give a sign, heard a bell ring, and in a very few minutes the mighty engines had stopped, and the ship came to a standstill. A small boat was lowered over the side of the great vessel and the man was rescued. Then the captain gave another sign, the bell rang

FAITH HEALING

again; and in another few minutes the engines were going full speed once more, and the ship resumed its journey as if no interruption had taken place. From this the boy learnt not only that the captain could stop the ship when he wanted to, but also that he did stop it when he thought there was sufficient reason.

Next morning the little girl was standing looking down into the engine room, when a large doll she was holding slipped from her grasp and fell into the whirling machinery. She began to cry, and was about to look for the captain, when her brother who had witnessed her loss said, "What's the use of going to the captain? The doll is probably crushed by the machinery. Besides, he'll have to stop the engines to get it. Why should he? A lost doll is not like a man overboard. And he'll probably tell you to be more careful with your doll."

The girl, however, had great confidence in the captain, and when she found him she said, "I'm sorry I dropped my doll. Do you think you can get it? I don't ask you to stop the engines, but do get it for me, if you can." The captain smiled and said he would see what could be done. It was not a very definite promise, but the girl was satisfied. The loss of a doll might not be a good reason for stopping the engines; yet the fact that the captain had halted the ship when the man fell overboard was sufficient reason for the girl to trust him in her own trouble.

The captain disappeared into the engine room, while the girl waited expectantly and the boy, skeptically. The engines did not stop, but at length the captain reappeared carrying the doll, not much the worse for its fall. The girl was grateful. But the boy, forgetting his philosophy, gave vent to envy. "Oh, yes," he complained, "the captain can take trouble over *your* doll, but he did not care when I lost my ball. He's not fair!" But

Healing and the Reign of Law

again the boy was wrong. When they went ashore at the end of the voyage, the captain surprised the boy by buying him a better ball than the one he had lost at sea.

A childish parable, you say. Yes, for it is a story about the childish perplexities of two children. Moreover, like all illustrations, it has its faults and limitations. But it has one point of value; it enables us to see that God is no more the slave of the universe than the captain is the slave of the machinery of the ship. Modern science has taught us to regard the universe as a great machine, working with the unfailing regularity of a ship's engines. It is thus an orderly and law-abiding scheme of things. Does that mean that God is a prisoner of His own laws? Is He so bound by His own creation that He cannot do anything in response to His children's cries, however much He may want to? We are told that spiritual healing involves miracles and miracles cannot happen in a law-abiding universe. But does it involve miracles in the sense of acting contrary to nature? The captain performed no miracle when he stopped the engines to rescue the man overboard. He used no miraculous powers when he went down to the engine room to recover the little girl's doll. No, he merely utilized his knowledge of natural law, which neither he nor anyone else could abrogate—or even "neutralize"—to realize a purpose he regarded as good and sufficient. Is the Ruler of the Universe less free than the captain of a ship?

Our American poet, James Russell Lowell, in one of his best-known poems, speaks of God standing "within the shadows, keeping watch above His own." It is not unlike the idea expounded by the old Scottish preacher Thomas Chalmers. He used to speak of God operating from "behind the scenes." Two theories of the relation of miracle to natural law can be deduced from this idea. The Living God interposes from "within the shadows"—from "behind the scenes"—not to set aside the natural order, but rather to supplement and control it. If the former, it would be the contravention, suspension, neutralization, of the order of nature—a theory which the scientific view of the universe could not possibly tolerate. But if the latter, then it would be the divine disposition of events within the natural order—a theory which religion cannot forego and which science could accept.

In this sense "belief in miracles stands simply for the position that if God is alive, He must reveal Himself in definite acts. A God merely postulated or inferred by the human mind does no miracles; He remains in silent inaction until man is kind enough to discover Him. The God of religious faith, on the other hand, stirs man out of inaction by His creative acts. . . . To believe in the living God and to believe in miracles are the same thing."[8]

It follows that the idea of the "reign of law," although a useful and necessary concept, is not adequate to signify the whole of reality. Science is concerned with the order of nature, and God's dealings through nature are always orderly. But it is God who controls the order, and not the order that controls God."[9]

7
Healers, Healing Missions and Healing Shrines

THE ART OF healing is as old as mankind—a fact we noted in our first chapter. Healers and their works have flourished in every age, from the days of primitive man right down to our own time. The rational—as opposed to the magical—approach to the problems of health and disease began with the Greek physician, Hippocrates. His work was a revolutionary step in the right direction, and it laid the foundations of modern medical practice. Since his day, save for some periods of stagnation and even regression, medicine has slowly become more scientific, until in our own country today medical knowledge and surgical skills have reached a high pitch of efficiency. So much has been done in preventing epidemics, like cholera and typhoid, in finding cures for such killing diseases as pneumonia and diphtheria, in developing new techniques, such as blood plasma and antibiotic drugs, that the life expectancy of the average American has been practically doubled since the turn of the century. Our immense debt to the great army of general practitioners, medical and surgical specialists, and research workers is beyond computation. And the future holds even greater promise.

FAITH HEALING

But far older than scientific medicine are the techniques used by those who follow other ways of healing. By their opponents these methods are frequently labelled "unscientific," but it might be nearer the mark to call them "non-scientific." The theories of the primitive witch doctor as to the origin and nature of disease and the methods to be used to combat sickness are very far removed from those of your family doctor, but that he had his successes cannot be disputed. And the same thing is true of the priest-physicians who haunted the Asclepian temples of the Graeco-Roman world.

In a somewhat loose sense the modern counterpart of these ancient healers is the present-day medico; but it would be nearer the mark to regard the unorthodox healer in every age as their real descendant. Perhaps the present-day psychiatrist and psychologist may also be classed as true offspring of the ancient healers, though they must not be spoken of as "unorthodox."

Of course, medicine itself was frequently unscientific, though quite orthodox, and its exponents unconscious quacks, though held in high esteem. In sixteenth- and seventeenth-century England the health and healing of the ordinary person were in the hands of apothecaries and barbers, who were respectively the physicians and surgeons of the time; they were invariably ignorant men, and their work was crude and cruel. (Trained doctors were relatively few in number and for the most part their services were confined to the upper classes.) Most of their remedies were folk remedies based on a mixture of herbalism and magic. A person bitten by a snake was urged to eat snake flesh and to anoint himself with snake fat. Viper flesh was also recommended as a cure for malignancy, and was used as the sovereign remedy for cancer, in medical circles, right into the eighteenth century. The medical textbooks of the

Healers, Missions and Healing Shrines

time contain the most curious prescriptions. One of these affirms that "essence of vipers is a most excellent medicine, dissolves all excrements and coagulations of humors, cleaning and purifying like soap ... so that, as it were, it even renovates a man, by taking away what is contrary to nature, and adding what is requisite." People who suffered "from skin growing over the eyes" were told to take the head of a coal-black cat, burn it to ashes in a new pot, and blow some of the ashes into the eyes every day. The cure for convulsions, epilepsy, and other nervous diseases could be obtained by wearing or chewing the rear right hoof of an elk. The sufferer could also rub his ear with it, or his heart, but it had to be done with the left hand, not the right. Herbalism and magic were involved in the cure for sciatica. The patient was to apply an ointment made from onions, neat's foot oil, and other ingredients, and then afterward wear, for sixteen days, "a cat's skin with the hairy side next to the flesh," after which "the part grieved shall find great ease thereby." As late as 1862 the celebrated Dr. John Hastings published a medical work entitled *The Value of Excreta of Reptiles in Phthisis and Other Diseases.*

These are typical of the remedies used in medical practice generally until the eighteenth century and some of them survived into the nineteenth. Probably a fair number of cures were effected, the curative agent being, however, not the concoction, but the psychological mechanism which we today know as "suggestion." No doubt, suggestion also plays an important part in present-day medicine—as witness the use of placebos and the recognized therapeutic value of faith in his doctor on the part of the patient. But beyond this, present-day medical knowledge is a marvelous inter-related body of knowledge—not complete or perfect, of course—based on the findings of the natural sciences, such as chemistry, biology, physiology, histology, and anatomy. "Let the facts speak" is the motto of modern medicine, as it is the motto of all the sciences; and scientific facts have been used to make clinical procedures more reliable. The structure of the human body is known; so is the way in which the various organs work; and so are many of the body's chemical and mechanical processes. The various diseases have been classified, and the course they take in the body has been charted. Thus the doctor, in many instances, can make a correct diagnosis, and in not a few cases can offer a reliable prognosis. Surely, this "noble army" of men and women, faithful to their ideals and devoted to their healing ministry, follow in the footsteps of the Great Physician!

What about the faith healers, of whom the modern world has seen quite a number? In the eighteenth century there were John Wesley, George Fox, and Valentine Greatrakes. In the following century there were Joseph Smith, G. O. Barnes, J. Alexander Dowie, and Mrs. Mary Baker Eddy. In our day we have the Rev. Oral Roberts, Pastor George Jeffries, Harry Price, Mrs. Agnes Sanford, Mrs. Elsie Salmon, the Rev. Alexander Holmes, together with a large company of little-known healers and the many practitioners licensed by the Board of the Church of Christ Scientist. The above-named were referred to in an earlier chapter. We may add here the name of Dorothea Trudel, a Swiss Protestant healer in the middle of the last century. She is reputed to have healed hundreds of people by her prayers in the years 1850-1860. She was brought to trial by the church authorities, in the village of Mannedorf. There is a legal record of the trial embodying the sworn testimony of many witnesses as to the reality of the cures.

All the above may be described as *religious* healers, but there is one twentieth-century practitioner who stands in a class by himself—Emile Coué, who died in 1926. He was not a medical man, but an apothecary turned psychologist. He initiated a "new way of ideas" in the treatment of the sick, and founded the New Nancy School of therapeutics. He is still remembered by most people as the originator of the famous formula: "Every day and in every way I am getting better and better." This was an excellent way to teach the man in the street "the power of positive thinking" and to make him realize a most important truth, the influence of mental states upon physical conditions. In a way, Coué anticipated the findings of what nowadays is called parapsychology, based on experiments into the facts and character of what is known as extra-sensory perception (symbolized by ESP). As the leading exponent of this new development in psychology puts it: "If mind can operate ever so little on objects such as rolling dice, it seems reasonable to suppose that it should be able to influence the matter of its own body."[1]

The French psychologist knew nothing about ESP experiments with dice and cards, but he was convinced that mental states have power over physical conditions. And he utilized this conviction in the healing of the sick. He believed in the therapeutic power of self-suggestion. By "suggestion" is meant the acceptance of an idea by the subconscious mind independent of the reasons for its acceptance. More briefly, it may be defined as "the subconscious realization of an idea."[2] There are two forms of suggestion: suggestion from without ("heterosuggestion") and suggestion from within ("autosuggestion"). Coué taught that only self-suggestion can work with any assurance of success, that to be effective heterosuggestion must first become autosuggestion.

This principle he applied to the healing of the sick. But the ideas subconsciously realized must be positive, not negative. The sickness must not be named, because it is a negative idea.

FAITH HEALING

And the thought of overcoming the illness must be couched in the present tense, not in the future. Nor must any act of will be involved. The patient must not say, "I *shall* get better" or "I *will* get better." What he must affirm is "I *am* getting better." Healing is thus not a question of will power, but of the imagination, and when the two come into conflict it is always the imagination that wins. Suggest to yourself that you are getting better and get better you will.

The idea was quite simple, but it worked. Coué had phenomenal success. The movement he started swept over Europe like a religious revival. In the course of a few years thousands of sick people visited his clinic at Nancy, and many most astounding cures were recorded. Thus this modest little Frenchman (there was nothing of the showman about him), by his work and teaching, paved the way for what in our time is known as "psychological healing."

The term "psychological healing" is, however, ambiguous, and can be misleading. It is usable in two senses, one narrow and the other wide. We use it in the narrow sense when we refer to the cure of mental disorders by psychiatric and psychotherapeutic techniques. These techniques are varied. The psychiatrist and clinical psychologist, in treating a patient suffering from a functional paralysis of the legs, may use hypnotic suggestion to effect a cure. Dr. James A. Hadfield, the famous British medical psychologist, is noted for this. A psychologist who is a disciple of Freud will in all likelihood dispense with hypnotism as being uncertain in its results, and will use the free association method, in which the patient is encouraged to talk out his problems and difficulties. He will be asked to relate his dreams so that the tangled skein of his unfulfilled wishes may be unravelled, and thus help toward a cure. There are other methods, too, like the word association test and the "ink-

Healers, Missions and Healing Shrines

blot" test, and even physical methods, such as the electric shock treatment and the insulin shock treatment; all of which are used to bring about mental healing. One authority has stated that the day will come when every home will have a family psychiatrist just as nowadays it has a family physician. This statement is probably an exaggeration, but it at least bears witness to both the need and the place of psychological healing in the world of today.

In the wide sense the phrase "psychological healing" is applied by many people to what happens in faith healing meetings. The fundamental question in this connection is: Are the seeming cures examples of spiritual healing or only of psychological relief? If the former, we can safely assume that they would be genuine and lasting cures; if the latter, then they might be only temporary phenomena. Millions of people today have become familiar with the religious mass meeting in which healing procedure is made to play a prominent part—thanks to the miracle of television.

Oral Roberts, in addition to being a very fluent speaker, has a magnetic personality. The type of service in which he is the central figure is supercharged with emotionalism, and expectation on the part of the vast congregation is immense. In such an atmosphere, and in such a context, the most amazing things can happen, as any psychologist will testify. Is it to be wondered at that Oral Roberts seems to cure functional disorders —hysterical deafness, hysterical stuttering, hysterical paralysis, and the like? Are any of these cures permanent? And are there any *medically proven* cases of the healing of organic diseases? And if any genuine healing takes place, is it the result of the workings of the Divine Spirit or is it the outcome of mass hypnotic suggestion? Or could it not be both are true and that mass hypnotic suggestion is God's way of working? Such

FAITH HEALING

questions are bound to crop up in connection with healing missions of this type.

Many who are quite in sympathy with the idea and practice of faith healing nevertheless regard the mass healing meeting as a danger to men's spiritual and emotional life. Dr. Leslie Weatherhead is one of them. So are the bishops who met in conference at Lambeth in 1920. One of the dangers Dr. Weatherhead sees is the loss of religious faith through the disillusionment that follows a temporary cure. In some of his writings he gives actual cases known to him personally of people who were supposedly healed instantaneously in the emotionally charged atmosphere of the mass meeting, but whose disability soon returned, and whose "last state was worse than the first." As for the Report of the Lambeth Conference (1920), the bishops say this: "On account of the immense importance we attach to the spiritual preparation of the individual, as well as for other reasons, we are not prepared to give any encouragement to public missions of healing."[3]

I myself have had a limited experience with these mass healing meetings—both in Britain and in our own country—but it has been sufficient to make me realize that there *are* real dangers involved in this type of gathering, even if some genuine cures can be chalked up; and watching Oral Roberts' spectacular "healing line" on television does nothing to correct that impression. I have also attended the kind of healing service from which all sensational elements are rigorously excluded. This latter kind of service is not usually overcrowded, probably not more than two hundred people being present. It is always conducted with dignity and reverence; and if the minister preaches a sermon or gives an address, it will be quiet and reasoned, and given without any "oratorical fireworks." The final act of the service will be prayer for the sick, together with the laying on of hands. About a score of afflicted folk will come to the front and kneel around the altar. The minister will go to each one separately, offering a prayer of intercession and placing his hands upon the patient's head. If any physical healings take place under such circumstances, I personally have not witnessed them. But I am sure that they do take place —on the testimony of those who have known of them— though the minister does not seek to exploit these cures for publicity purposes. Dr. Weatherhead would probably have no objection to this kind of service; and he certainly believes in public congregational prayer for the sick. But he prefers that the laying on of hands be done in private, in the patient's own room, or in the minister's office, or in some small chapel, with only truly interested and deeply concerned friends present.

What about healing shrines? Hundreds of them existed in the ancient world, the most popular being the Temple of Asclepius at Epidauris, in Greece. There are not a few in our time, such as Holywell in North Wales, and St. Anne de Beaupré, in Quebec, Canada. The most famous of modern healing shrines is, of course, Lourdes, in the South of France. In 1858 a fourteen-year-old peasant girl, Bernadette Soubirous, reported that she had had eighteen visions of the Blessed Virgin, who assured her that a healing spring would gush up at that very spot. Sure enough the spring appeared, and it has increased in volume until at the present time it gives over 26,000 gallons a day. The water has been chemically analyzed, and it shows that it has the same composition as the other water in that region; it has no medicinal properties.

In the near century since the shrine was established it has been visited by several million sick and afflicted persons. Many cures have been claimed, but only forty-nine have been approved as miracles by the ecclesiastical authorities, nine of them in the last ten years. These are all cures of organic disorders, including cancer of the tongue, breast malignancy, congenital deafness, ulcerated leg of twelve years' standing, compound fracture of the leg of eight years' duration, tubercular disease of the spine, a club foot, bow legs, and others.

Functional disorders are not included in the record of cures, for it is freely admitted by the Lourdes medical authorities that the curative agent could be nothing more than heightened suggestion. And that could be devoid of religious significance. Many of the people who are thus cured—and 4000 is the number alleged for the first fifty years of the shrine's existence, probably an exaggerated reckoning—do not believe in any form of religion, whereas many of those who are not cured are devout and earnest Catholics. It would seem that often the unbeliever is healed, and the believer unhealed. And those who were healed of their functional and nervous disabilities need not have taken the journey to the Shrine of Our Lady of Lourdes. They could have been cured by a visit to M. Coué's modest parlor-clinic at Nancy or as the result of treatment by a competent psychotherapist in their home town.

Nevertheless, there are many well-attested cases of organic cures amongst the pilgrims to Lourdes. There is the case of François de Lavaur, who for a dozen years suffered with leg ulcers, and was cured in one night by the application of compresses steeped in water from the Lourdes pool. The three doctors who attested the healing said that it was "a most extraordinary fact, and indeed supernatural." There is the case of Raymond Caral. Dr. Boissarie diagnosed a skin eruption of the face as malignant; he was quite certain of it. Yet the patient was cured in eight days by bathing his cancerous face in the water of Lourdes, leaving nothing but a scar that could hardly be noticed. And there is the case of the deaf mute, a girl who had never heard or spoken from birth. At the age of twenty she visited Lourdes and put a few drops of the "holy water" in her ears on three successive days. Suddenly she was able to hear and to make sounds (she had to learn gradually, by imitation, how to pronounce words). The family doctor, who examined her after the event, wrote: "From earliest infancy this young girl, who was placed under my care, offered every symptom of natal deaf-mutism.... On her return from a pilgrimage to Lourdes she instantly recovered the faculty of hearing. The cure is certain and undeniable. The deaf and dumb girl can hear and speak."

These three cures were achieved through physical contact with the Holy Water, but that this is not essential is proved by the fact that healings have taken place where water from the grotto has not been used. A man suffering from incurable glaucoma, visited the grotto and attended a novena. He was completely cured. He afterward reported: "I write and read as much as I want to, without spectacles, without precautions, without effort, without fatigue"—a report confirmed by the attending physicians, including the oculist who first diagnosed the disease. There is the still more remarkable case of Jeanne Fretel. She had been ill for ten years, most of the time being confined to hospital, and for the last three years she had been completely bed-ridden. Three times in a period of five years she received Extreme Unction. The doctors diagnosed her malady as incurable tubercular peritonitis, with additional meningitic complications. She arrived at Lourdes competely prostrate. She took part in Mass for the Sick, in the course of which she suddenly felt better. Later she was able to sit upright for the first time, and an hour later was given a solid meal such as she had not eaten for years. Next day Jeanne Fretel went to the Lourdes Medical Bureau, where she demonstrated her

FAITH HEALING

ability to walk despite almost complete atrophy of the leg muscles. A thorough medical examination showed that all pathological symptoms had entirely gone. In the weeks that followed she ate and slept well, and gained steadily in weight. Two years later, in a letter to the bureau, she wrote that she was in perfect health and working very hard as a nurse. Other cures—mostly of functional disorders—have occurred without coming into contact with water from the sacred spring. Patients witness the Procession of the Host or visit the Stations of the Cross or take part in a Mass for the Sick (as Jeanne Fretel did) and the "miracle of healing" takes place.

Our Lady of Lourdes is not remarkable for the number of cures effected at the Sacred Shrine, because the number is about two per cent. But it is remarkable for the great care taken to adjudicate and evaluate every alleged cure. There is a well-organized medical bureau which studies the patient's case *before* the visit to Lourdes, as well as *during* and *after* the visit. Any cure claimed is also examined by the Association of Lourdes Doctors, which has more than 5000 members; and further investigation is undertaken by the International Medical Commission, consisting of one hundred physicians from many nations. If these three investigating groups of doctors are of the opinion that a cure bears on it the stamp of the miraculous it is reported to the ecclesiastical authorities for their final judgment. Mental and nervous cases are thus eliminated, and fraudulent claims thrown out. The medical bureau has reported twelve hundred cases as having a claim to be classed as miracles of physical healing, but the theologians have put their stamp of approval on only forty-nine.

In 1949 Dr. Weatherhead made a visit to Lourdes to observe at firsthand the procedures and the results. He was deeply impressed by what he saw, though—because of the rarity of the cures—he would hesitate to recommend that any sick person make the pilgrimage. Nevertheless, he does not hesitate to add this: "In my opinion, there can be no possible doubt that the cures of physical illness take place in a remarkable way."[4] How are these cures effected? Perhaps the statement of F. W. H. Myers, in his great work on *Human Personality,* comes as near to an explanation as any. "It is *not* true," he says, "a thousand times *not* true, that a bottle of water from a spring near which a girl saw an hallucinatory figure will by miraculous virtue heal a Turk in Constantinople; but *it is true that on some influx from the unseen world*—an influence dimly adumbrated in that Virgin figure and that sanctified water—depends the life and energy of this everyday world."[5] The divine breaks through into human life, yet without breaking any law which expresses the Divine Nature. We may think a law is broken, and call what happens a "miracle," but that is only because we have not yet discovered what that law is.

8 Healing and Human Personality

HUMAN PERSONALITY HAS two fundamental aspects, the material and the immaterial. These two aspects form a still more fundamental unity which is broken only at death. "Material" has a fairly clear-cut meaning, since it stands for the body, and we all know what our bodies are. But the terms used to describe the immaterial side of our constitution are apt to be confusing. We speak of "mind" and "soul" and "spirit." Sometimes they are regarded as synonymous, standing for one and the same entity. Sometimes only two of them are thought of as identical—"mind" and "soul," or "mind" and "spirit," or "soul" and "spirit." When only two of these terms are regarded as synonymous it is generally taken to mean that human personality has three basic constituents, the physical, the mental (also termed the psychological and the psychical), and the spiritual. In the interest of clarity this is a convenient view to accept. Thus we can say that man's nature is threefold, consisting basically of body, mind and spirit (or soul). The body is wholly physical, the spirit is wholly spiritual, whereas the mind partakes of the nature of both. A good example of the latter is seen in the emotions. Psychologists define an emotion as a stirred-up state of mind, but they point out too that it is also a perturbed condition of the body. As a feeling it belongs to the sphere of the mental, but inasmuch as it cannot exist without bodily manifestations it also belongs to the sphere of the physical. This can be clearly seen in the case, say, of fear. You are confronted with a dangerous situation. You feel afraid, and this is mental. But, in addition, your body trembles, your face goes white, your heart beats faster, your pulse races, and you make escape movements; these are all physical. They are two necessary aspects of one and the same experience; you cannot have the one without the other.

The medical profession—despite a lingering materialism of standpoint and practice—is more and more acknowledging the fact that body and mind constitute a unity in both health and disease. The rise of psychosomatic medicine bears witness to this, though probably "psychosomatic" is only a new term for some old insights. Furthermore, the prominence accorded nowadays to psychiatry and psychotherapy shows that the medicos as a whole have come to realize that physical healing is not enough, that psychological illnesses also call for skilled attention. More than one prominent physician has declared that at least half the people who come to him complaining of bodily ailments have nothing wrong with them physically, and that their troubles are wholly within the realm of the mind. And in many cases where there is actually organic disability the causative factor is perhaps to be found in some mental disturbance. But even if that were disputed, it cannot be denied that psychological factors can give rise to ailments that have the appearance of being physical. Blindness and deafness, abdominal tumors and limb paralysis, even pregnancy, can be simulated by the body as the result of purely mental illness.

Two general types of sickness, therefore, are now widely recognized by the medical profession, physical and psychological. Corresponding to these are two general kinds of healing procedures, those appertaining to the body and those appertaining to the mind. The former are practiced by the physician and the surgeon, the latter by the psychiatrist and the psychotherapist. But there is also a third kind of healing, with its own peculiar techniques,[1] co-ordinate with the other two, spiritual healing. Most doctors, being conservative by training, if not by nature, refuse to accept it as such, preferring to regard it as an unscientific delusion. Such cures as they are bound grudgingly to admit they assert to be cures of purely hysterical complaints, and even such instances they think can be explained along psychological lines. The great French psychologist, Pierre Janet, was very skeptical on this matter of spiritual healing. He wrote a massive two-volume treatise on *Psychological Healing,* a truly great work, in which he canvasses every aspect of the subject. Scientific honesty compels him to admit that the healing of organic maladies does take place at Lourdes; he even cites several undeniable cases. But he maintains that the cures are effected through the operation of psychological laws which we do not as yet fully understand. He lays great store on the fact of suggestion; the patient must be highly suggestible, and the suggestions given must be of the right quality and presented in the most effective manner.

Dr. Alexis Carrel, on the other hand, is a firm believer in spiritual healing. He is equally as famous as a scientist as Pierre Janet, and is far better known to our generation. Moreover, as a medical man and a research scientist he would know more about the organic aspects of the problem than does one whose speciality was the realm of mind. He admits that "miraculous cures" are relatively rare, but of the fact that people organically sick are healed as the result of someone praying he has not the slightest doubt; and it was an impartial investi-

Healing and Human Personality

gation of the Lourdes phenomena that helped him to come to this conviction. His own words are worth quoting: "Our present conception of the influence of prayer upon pathological lesions is based upon the observation of patients who have been cured almost instantaneously of various affections, such as peritoneal tuberculosis, cold abscesses, osteitis, suppurating wounds, lupus, cancer, etc. The process of healing changes little from one individual to another. Often an acute pain. Then a sudden sensation of being cured. In a few seconds, a few minutes, at the most a few hours, wounds are cicatrised, pathological symptoms disappear, appetite returns. Sometimes functional disorders vanish before the anatomical lesions are repaired. The skeletal deformations of Pott's disease, the cancerous glands, may still persist two or three days after the healing of the main lesions. The miracle is chiefly characterised by an extreme acceleration of the processes of organic repair. There is no doubt that the rate of cicatrisation of the anatomical defects is much greater than the normal one. The only condition indispensable to the occurrence of the phenomenon is prayer."[2]

Ultimately, of course, all healing is spiritual, since every cure comes from God, who is the Source of Light and Life and Love, the Fountain of Health and Holiness and Wholeness. In all applications of the therapeutic art men are "workers together with God" (to use St. Paul's phrase), even when they are not aware of it; indeed, even when, in a mood of unbelief, they refuse to acknowledge it. More and more members of the medical profession are losing their skepticism on this point, though they may not be fully persuaded as to the reality of spiritual healing. The doctor, in treating his patients, obeys some laws which he understands, and also some which he does not know. In the former case he may sense that—as

Kepler the famous astronomer used to say—he is "thinking God's thoughts after him." In the latter he is more of a seeker than a finder, yet he may feel that God is at work, though he does not as yet see the way of His doings.[3]

But while we say that all healing is ultimately spiritual, we find it convenient to distinguish spiritual healing from the physical and the psychotherapeutic. Furthermore, we ought to be clear as to this important fact—spiritual healing is not simply the cure of functional or organic diseases through the use of extra-physical and extra-psychological procedures. That is only a part of it. Spiritual healing is really the healing of the total personality, the whole man who is a unity of body, mind, and spirit. It is not merely the healing of the body or the healing of the mind by such specifically spiritual procedures as intercessory prayer. The healing of the spirit is also involved. Frequently this is the prior need, and the first thing to be looked for by both the healer and the patient is not physical restoration, but spiritual renewal. This is clearly suggested in the Gospel story of the young man who was paralyzed and who was brought to Christ on a kind of stretcher carried by four friends. Our Lord's first word to the poor fellow was, "Son, be of good cheer; thy sins be forgiven thee," and this was followed by, "Arise, take up thy bed, and go unto thine house" (Matthew 9:2, 6). That the patient—who was a sinner as well as a sufferer, and a sufferer because he was a sinner—was afflicted with a deep-rooted sense of guilt is clear.

It also seems to be suggested that the paralysis was, in some sense, the consequence of his sin. Hence Christ joined the two liberating words together, though putting "first things first." Spiritual renewal preceded and paved the way for physical restoration. The man rose from the stretcher and walked away, carrying the stretcher with him. No wonder the onlookers were amazed, and as Mark puts it, "glorified God, saying, We never saw it on this fashion." But even if no physical results had followed, the paralyzed man would have been made whole in his spirit, and—if religion means anything—that means that the healing most needed and desirable had been accomplished. The young man, no doubt, would have been disappointed, but it would have been a disappointment devoid of the bitterness that could have further afflicted his body.

Many people have had the experience of this man and have been cured in body and mind through the power of God working in wondrous ways and according to laws the meaning and nature of which we do not as yet understand. On the other hand, there are many people to whom physical healing has not come, but who rejoice in the experience of spiritual renewal. The "guilt complex" has been removed, and the assurance of restored fellowship with God has come to them, but the paralysis—or whatever their ailment may be—has remained. The fact of failure is a sore problem to us all. We do not know why, in some instances, the cure comes "by faith" or through prayer or as the outcome of a pilgrimage to some healing shrine and not in others. It may be because we do not yet know the laws that are involved in spiritual healing; or it may be that in many cases the conditions of healing are not fulfilled because they are not really known.

The fact that faith healing techniques often fail of the desired result is no argument against using them. Modern medicine has its failures too. The most skilful surgeon sometimes loses a patient, even in conditions when success has been confidently and honestly predicted. As for the so-called "miracle drugs," there are patients on whom they have no effect. But we do not discount modern medicine and surgery because of the failures. Why then should we refuse to make use of the

FAITH HEALING

methods of spiritual healing? It is true that in medicine and surgery the successes outweigh the failures many times over, and that with respect to faith healing and spiritual healing there are many more failures than there are successes. But go back a hundred years or so, to the days of the apothecary and the surgeon-barber, and what is the story then where the doctors were concerned? Since then the therapeutic art, both physical and psychological, has made great strides, and will make many more. Perhaps the same will be true of spiritual healing. There is much evidence to the effect that we are on the threshold of a great new era of spiritual power, that men are feeling the impact of a fresh spiritual impulse, and that one of the features will be greater success in the realm of spiritual healing because of a greater understanding of the laws of the spirit.

Spiritual healing, of part of the human personality or the whole of it, is possible because man is a spiritual being. He has affinities with the lower creatures, but he himself is more than an animal. He is a mechanical contrivance "fearfully and wonderfully made," but he is more than a machine. There is within him that which can enter into communion with the Eternal Spirit from whom all things proceed. He is permeated by spiritual perception and spiritual purpose far more than he usually realizes. The unity of body-mind and spirit is a unity in which spirit is the dominant partner. Indeed, the relationship between them is somewhat analogous to the relationship between the violinist and the violin. It is the relationship between the agent and the instrument. And this means that the spirit is the real self, the agent that uses the instrument, body-mind. Plato expressed this point of view aptly when he said that it is not our eyes that see, but we who see through them; that it is not our ears that hear, but we who hear by means of them.

The spiritual part of man is the regulative principle of the

Healing and Human Personality

whole. The spirit indwells body and mind, and uses them; apart from spirit they have no real life in their own right. To affirm this fundamental fact does not mean that we disparage body and mind. Does the violinist despise his violin? Nor do we discount physical harmony and mental fitness. The old Roman motto sums up a modern ideal as well: *Mens sana in corpore sano*—"a sound mind in a sound body." But does not the full realization of this ideal call for a "sound spirit" interpenetrating and regulating both?

It is because man is a spiritual being capable of communion with the Eternal Spirit that spiritual healing is possible. Even if no cases of such healing had ever been reported it would not be illogical to conclude that, because of the spiritual relationship between God and man, spiritual cures could be effected if only we knew how to bring them about. Furthermore, it is because man's spirit is the dominant factor in the body-mind-spirit unity, interpenetrating and regulating the other two factors, that spiritual healing need not be the healing of the spirit only, important though that be. There is plenty of evidence that the healing of bodily ailments is an actuality, and not merely a possibility (as previous chapters have shown). But it is not merely a matter of so-called "miraculous cures." There are many people who would not lay claim to such a spectacular experience, but who can testify to the fact that for them remarkable increments of religious faith and spiritual insight have meant an extraordinary sense of bodily and mental fitness. The experience has given them greatly increased physical and psychical vitality. In fact, it has seemed to them as if the very "texture" of personality had been completely transformed. Emotional warps were untangled, psychological patterns re-oriented, and even body cells profoundly influenced.

It is clear, therefore, that the spiritual healing of body and

FAITH HEALING

mind is possible because man's spirit can make its impact on the other two aspects of the human personality. We do not know just how this is done, but we do know that it is done. After all, we do not know how mind influences body and *vice versa,* but we have plenty of evidence that they do. Take such a simple thing as seeing an object, say, a television program. Light vibrations from the picture tube strike the retinas of the eyes, where they set up a nerve impulse which is carried along the appropriate nerve fibers until it reaches the visual nerve centers located in the occipital area at the back of the head. Then we see the picture that appears on the television screen. The light vibrations to the eyes, and the nerve impulse, are both physical, but our perception of the seen object is a mental state. How is the physical converted into the mental? How does the material impinge on the immaterial? The answer given by Aristotle 2000 years ago, by T. H. Huxley in the last century, and by the great British neurologist and physiologist, Sir Charles Sherrington today, is that we do not know.

Or take something that seems to be more mystifying, the phenomenon of hypnotism.[4] What hypnotism really is is still a debatable point among psychologists, but we do know that it is a mental process and that it produces physical results. The case of that "wonderful and curious little man," St. Francis of Assisi, is well known. By a process of self-hypnotism he reproduced in his body the stigmata, the five bleeding wounds of Christ. Hypnotic suggestion (and suggestion is the central operating factor in hypnosis) can produce in the body of suggestible persons, not only blisters and swellings and skin rashes, but also symptoms of hysteria, such as functional paralysis and functional blindness. Indeed, hypnotism has been used in surgery as a drugless anesthetic. The great Scottish surgeon, Dr. James Esdaile, used hypnosis to produce both general and

Healing and Human Personality

local anesthesia in his patients. He performed thousands of operations—many of them major operations, including leg amputations—in which the only anesthetic used was hypnotic suggestion. Perhaps it would be in common use today were it not for the fact that chemical anesthetics are more reliable and more easily administered. But the fact that the *mental* process of hypnotic suggestion is able to do these things, and that it is capable of being used as an anesthetic, shows that the mind *can* influence *physical* conditions.

It shows *can,* but it does not show *how.* The *how* is beyond our comprehension in the present state of our knowledge (or should we say "the present state of our ignorance"?), and may always be beyond our grasp. But we do not deny the reality of the reciprocal influence of the body-mind relationship because the *nexus* between them is inconceivable. Why then should we deny that man's spirit can make a healing impact on the two other aspects of personality because the mode of operation and the point of contact are beyond our ken? Even a casual review of the facts should convince any but the most hardened skeptic that spiritual healing is no mere chimera. The materials for a sound judgment are not scanty, but abundant to the point of embarrassment.

Twenty-four centuries ago Hippocrates taught that ill health is the outcome of physical disturbance, that in its essential nature disease consisted in a want of balance of the four cardinal body fluids. The want of balance concept, which has never been completely lost, has been resuscitated in our day and is coming very much to the front. With Hippocrates it was purely a physical concept, but with the modern physician it is psychophysical, that is, having reference to mind as well as to body. It does not give credence to the "four humors" of Hippocrates, but it is much concerned with the function of the ductless or endocrine glands in relation to physical and mental fitness. In this view the essential ingredient in health is that of balance. "A sound mind in a sound body," interpenetrated and regulated by a sound spirit, is not a mere static condition, but a dynamic ongoing of life in a harmonious and balanced way.

If this be true then it follows that the matter of health and ill health is not just the question of the absence or presence of certain microbes or poisons, but the more significant one of the human personality's ability to react to them in such a way that the individual's life can go forward unafflicted by the curse of disharmony and imbalance.

A further consideration follows from this, that the fundamental question confronting every one of us is not our psycho-physical-spiritual condition at any given moment, but the direction in which life is moving. Oliver Wendell Holmes's familiar saying applies here: "It is not where a man stands, but the direction in which he moves, that counts." Does not religion, as well as medicine, have a part to play in this? Is not faith in God as important, in this matter, as faith in one's physician? Are not the "means of grace" (as our fathers called prayer and worship, Bible reading and the sacraments) as effective in their way as the techniques of the medical profession? The procedures by which the spirit of man can make contact with the Reality we call God can have effects far beyond the spiritual side of the human personality. Spectacular cures wrought in mass revival meetings, or at sacred shrines, capture the popular imagination, but we usually forget to take account of the fact that religious worship—Protestant, Catholic, Jewish, or any other form—is a mighty factor in maintaining that wholeness or balance in which good health essentially consists. The therapeutic value of normal acts of worship is gen-

Healing and Human Personality

erally passed unnoticed, but that this value is real and significant can hardly be questioned. Acts of worship enable the sincere worshiper to face the facts of life squarely and to react to them in a health-creating manner. This, of course, is true not only of religion, but also of medicine and psychotherapy.

On some of the preceding pages the words "suggestion" and "faith" have been used. They are terms of utmost importance in any discussion of healing by nonphysical methods. The words are often confused, not only by people in general but also by some of those who write about spiritual healing. People frequently speak of "faith cures" when they are referring to what should be called "suggestion cures," and so give a religious turn to something that could have no religious significance whatsoever. For "suggestion" stands for a psychological mechanism, whereas "faith" means a religious exercise. Of course, faith in its secular or nonreligious sense is demanded in mental healing. Speaking of psychoanalysis, Dr. W. H. H. Rivers says that its whole procedure "is calculated to bring into play the agencies of faith and suggestion."[5] Yes, but the faith thus brought into play is not necessarily religious faith. It could be that, of course, if the analysis were being made by a psychiatrist who was himself a deeply religious man, such as Drs. William Brown, James A. Hadfield, or H. Crighton Miller. But it need not be religious faith, and in very many cases it is not.

Yet faith in the secular sense must be involved in both physical and psychological healing. The patient must believe in his physician and his recommendations and remedies; he must have complete confidence in the surgeon who is going to operate; he must have faith in the psychotherapist if the treatment is to be successful. Faith is thus the ground of suggestion and suggestibility, which are of some importance in physical healing, but which become of prime significance in the healing of mental illness. As the Swiss psychiatrist, Dubois, puts it: "The nervous (i.e., neurotic) patient is on the way to health as soon as he has the conviction that he can be cured; he is to be considered cured on the day that he thinks himself cured."[6] But this conviction depends again upon faith—in the nonreligious sense—in the person of the healer and in the treatment he gives. And this kind of faith seems to be involved at all levels of healing from the simplest physical treatment to the most complicated psychoanalytical procedure.

It has been said that the virtue of faith lies in the virtue of its object. If that be true then religious faith is faith in God, and Christian faith is faith in the God who has revealed Himself supremely and savingly in Christ. Religious faith is more than mere belief, though of course it involves belief. It is rather the exercise of the total personality as knowing, feeling, and willing. Thus it is an activity of what the older psychologists were accustomed to speak of as cognition, affection, and conation. These are the three ultimate constituents of consciousness; and faith is an activity of all three. Such an activity is directed toward the Eternal Spirit. It is an attitude of active confidence in Him whom we spiritually apprehend to be the Source and Sustainer of all created being. But its Object is not some vague Principle, not some inanimate Power, but a Being who is Personal—or, at least, is not less than personal. Religious faith is therefore a personal relationship, a relationship between two persons, God and man, in which the power of the One comes to the rescue of the other.

What about its place and function in spiritual healing? That is not an easy question to answer. We know that faith does operate in the curing of disease, though we do not know how it does. It is a kind of channel through which the healing

Healing and Human Personality

energy of the divine flows. But we also know that frequently no healing comes, even though faith is exercised. In the healing miracles of the Gospel we see that faith in Christ as Healer was the prime prerequisite. "Thy faith hath saved thee; go in peace" is the formula that seems to fit every cure, except perhaps the casting out of demons. It is not suggested that our Lord ever failed to effect a cure, but we are led to believe that in the absence of a vital faith He refused to exercise His healing powers; again with the possible exception of demonic possession. This is not the case with us today in our faith-healing efforts. There are people who are healed without faith, and there are people with faith who are not healed. It is not impossible that some people have an *unconscious* faith in Christ. That this is not so unlikely as may be supposed at first sight may be judged from Christ's parable of the Grand Assize (Matthew 25:31-46). The righteous were those who performed deeds of mercy for their needy fellows, but *did not know that they were doing it for Him*. They thought they were serving men only, and their faith in Christ was unconscious. The latter may also include those who apparently have no faith in Christ, and no belief in religion, but are nevertheless cured. Hence there is no intractable problem here.

But there is a problem of considerable dimensions in the case of the faithful who are not healed, however earnestly they may pray for themselves or others may pray for them. It may be that other factors are involved of which we know nothing or at which we can only guess. And it may be further that spiritual healing will advance to greater successes in due time just as medicine and surgery have made substantial advances during the past half century or so. Meanwhile, we recognize that there are many saintly and devout people to whom no methods —spiritual, psychological, or physical—have brought healing,

FAITH HEALING

and who have learned to know something of "the patience of unanswered prayer." Of course, they are disappointed. They would not be human otherwise. But they are not bitter and sour. They have not lost their faith in the goodness and justice of God. They continue to pray and to hope, for others as well as themselves. They are living examples of faith as "the soul's insight or discovery of some Reality that enables a man to stand anything that can happen to him in the universe."[7] And, for a time at least, it has to be said:

> The answer he got to the prayer he made,
> Was power to see the thing through.[8]

9 Healing: Quest for a Lost Faith

IN THAT WONDERFUL self-portraiture of our Lord which is recorded in the Fourth Gospel Christ speaks of Himself, among other things, as being the Good Shepherd. The suggestion is not so much that men are like sheep (though they often are in spiritual things), but that He is the One who cares for them and shepherds them in every way that is needful. That self-portraiture of Jesus is expressed in what has been called the "Sevenfold 'I am,'" beginning with "I am the bread of life" and concluding with "I am the resurrection and the life."[1] It is perhaps somewhat surprising that our Lord did not also say "I am the great physician." Yet He did claim that lovely title indirectly. He did so when, defending His attitude towards sinners and tax-gatherers against the criticisms of the religious leaders, He said, "They that be whole need not a physician, but they that are sick." He did so again when He said to His astonished hearers in the synagogue at Nazareth, "Ye will surely say unto me this proverb, Physician, heal thyself."

But what is more to the point is that He showed by His many "mighty deeds" of compassion that He was in truth the Great Physician. True, the primary objective of His ministry was to restore the lost children of God to their Heavenly

FAITH HEALING

Father. But He who "knew what was in man" was not unmindful of the fact that the constitution of human nature involved the physical and the mental, as well as the spiritual. That is why His ministry was not merely the "cure of souls"; it was also the healing of sick bodies and deranged minds. It would seem that Christ regarded man's mortal enemy as being not one, but two. The arch-enemy, of course, is moral evil, the essence of which is the alienation of man's immortal spirit from the Eternal Spirit; and it was to bring about the reconciliation of God and man—to remove the alienation—that He lived and died. But there was another enemy against which He directed His mighty strength: sickness of mind and body. It was not merely a "passion for *souls*" that motivated His "labor of love," it was compassion for *men*—for the *whole* man as body-mind and spirit. Thus His ministry had a double aspect. First and foremost He aimed at spiritual renewal. But in addition to this—indeed, as part of it—He sought to give men release from their bodily ills and their mental distresses.

His followers in all ages, therefore, have always regarded the title the Great Physician as pre-eminently applicable to Him. On this point we Christians are of one mind. Further, we agree that the Master commanded His immediate disciples to heal the sick and to cast out devils, and that the Gospel record assures us that this command was successfully obeyed. Still further, we see from the Acts of the Apostles that this healing commission was faithfully carried out in the early years of the Christian movement. It seems that power to heal was not withdrawn from the church when our Lord vanished into the Unseen. But at this point agreement ends. Catholics, pointing to the many stories of miracles performed by the saints over the first fifteen centuries of the Church's history, and to the wonder-cures at Lourdes and other healing shrines in our own

Healing: Quest for a Lost Faith

day, maintain that Christ's healing power is still abroad in the world. Protestants, on the other hand, at the Reformation, rejected the "cult of the saints" and the miracles that went with it; and even today—a time when there is an awakened interest in the possibilities of faith healing—most non-Catholic Christians are not impressed by stories of miraculous cures, past or present. Classical Protestantism does not, of course, deny the reality of the Biblical miracles, and certainly not the "mighty deeds" of Christ. And some contemporary Protestants—those accepting what may be termed, without offense, the traditional theology—believe that our Lord's healing commission was fulfilled by the Church well into the fifth century, or at least into the third century, and for this view they can cite no less an authority than Harnack. Besides, there are Protestants—most of them belonging to what are called the "fringe sects" (again without offense), such as the Assemblies of God—who are sure that spiritual healing is the duty of the modern Church and that this duty is being performed by all those preachers who are presenting to this present age what St. Paul called "all the counsel of God."

Nevertheless, the general Protestant attitude is to discount the so-called "ecclesiastical miracles" (the Reformers maintained that they were either figments of the imagination or the works of the devil) and to believe that the power to heal the sick by other than non-miraculous methods disappeared at the close of the Apostolic Age. And the argument at the back of this view is that the healing miracles were no longer needed to validate the genuineness of Christianity or to aid it in its conflicts with an unbelieving world—a rather curious consideration when it is remembered that most of the Church's toughest battles, both intellectually and practically, were fought in the sub-Apostolic Age and the centuries immediately following. Coupled with this view, and sometimes confused with it, is the belief that the power to work miracles was early withdrawn, not because it was no longer needed, but because of a sort of collapse in the inner life of the Church. The faith of Christ's followers lost its dynamic force. It was but a pale reflection of the mighty power we see in the Gospels and in the Acts of the Apostles, incapable of doing the "greater works" which the Master promised His disciples would be able to accomplish. Harnack seems to suggest this when he says: "As proofs of 'the Spirit and of power' subsided after the beginning of the third century, the extraordinary moral tension also became relaxed, paving the way gradually for a morality which was adapted to a worldly life."[2] Apparently the Church gradually lost faith in its inherited methods of healing the sick—by intercessory prayer, the laying on of hands, and anointing with oil—in favor of nonreligious methods of healing which it learned through contact with Greek culture. This though for centuries the Church continued to maintain an order of official exorcists, possibly a sort of continuance of the New Testament methods. There are, however, contemporary theologians who cannot accept this "lost faith" hypothesis. The Scottish writer John Porteous speaks for a large company when he writes: "We cannot think miracles passed away because of a failure of faith. They were the very kind of thing that faith was likely to hold on to. They passed away because their purpose was served. Most of the miracles (if not all) of later times are suspect, as being usually associated with gross superstition, or with eccentric doctrines. The 'new psychology' can give a sufficient account of such of them as are not delusions."[3] This, it may be added, is the explanation of most "modernist" Christians; many of them go so far as to deny the nature miracles of Christ Himself and to assert that His healing miracles can be explained solely in psychological terms.

Healing: Quest for a Lost Faith

Did the power to accomplish miracles of healing entirely disappear after, say, the first two centuries of the Church's history? Catholics say that it did not. But even they have to admit that something did happen to the Church's healing ministry. If the power to work healing miracles did not entirely vanish, it came more and more to be associated with holy persons and sacred places—with saints and shrines—and less and less a part of the Church's general life. These deeds became the normal accompaniment of the lives of the saints and thus the abnormal accompaniment of the life of the Church. No wonder superstition, myth and legend ran riot. Even today one of the conditions to be fulfilled before any Church figure can be canonized is an affirmative answer to the question: "Has he (or she) any healing miracles to his (or her) credit?"

And was this power withdrawn because of lack of faith? Did the ability to work miracles of healing disappear because of some failure in the inner life of the Church? Was the loss of this power the penalty for compromising with the world? The Church gained increasingly in political influence and financial security; was the price paid for this the loss of power to preach the Gospel and heal the sick? Whatever the answer it is certain that the Church of post-apostolic centuries was sorely lacking in the things that made the Church of the Apostles a mighty force in the world. Even such miracles as were performed were interpreted differently from the New Testament point of view. They were regarded as signs of divine favor to certain persons of extreme sanctity. Their value lay in the fact that they proved the divine origin of the Catholic Church, instead of in the fact that they were expressions of God's loving concern for man. The healing miracles of the Gospels are an acted proclamation of God's love; the healing miracles of the post-apostolic Church are rather a demonstration of His mighty power; and, we may add, a power exercised not primarily on behalf of suffering men, but in the interests of an ecclesiastical organization.

It would seem as if the healing miracles of the New Testament did not survive the Age of the Apostles, that such wonders as did occur were of a lower spiritual quality. And if healing miracles of the quality and character of those ascribed to Christ in the Gospels—and of most of those recorded in the Acts of the Apostles—did finally cease, the question arises: Was this the divine intention? When our Lord said, "Heal the sick," was this command given only to twelve apostles and to the seventy disciples, and through them to their immediate successors? As recorded in the Fourth Gospel, Christ said to His followers: ". . . He that believeth on me, the works that I do shall he do also; and *greater works than these shall he do* . . ." (John 14:12). What did He mean by "greater works"? And did He give it as a promise of tremendous power to all His disciples for all time? The late Dr. A. J. Gossip calls it "a breath-taking promise." And he adds: "The confident promise of this verse seems on the face of it incredible. If this is even remotely possible, then we have never taken in what Christ has in his heart for us, and have been satisfied with much less than what he has planned to give us." Then follows a beautiful homily on the glorious achievements of Christ's followers all down through the ages. "Take out of our human story all that has been effected since he died by those whom he inspired and helped, and how its glory would be dimmed, and what a mass of heroism, devotion, gallantry, endurance, achievement would be lost to us! And the tale runs on and on and on. In his own day Christ made only a passing impression on his own little atomy of a land, and almost none on the great world beyond it. But the followers of his have swept across the earth like the conquerors they are, winning masses for the Master, far more than he ever gained himself."[4] All this

Healing: Quest for a Lost Faith

—and the rest of the comment Dr. Gossip offers—is beautiful and true. But not a single reference is made to Christ's healing miracles. Apparently the famous preacher did not believe that our Lord was thinking of His "mighty deeds" when He spoke of "greater works than these."

The same is almost—but not quite—true of the comment of another Scottish divine, Dr. Marcus Dods. In his exposition of Christ's "breath-taking promise" he refers to the miracles of healing, but interprets this word of the Master in such a way as to suggest that it could not mean that the disciples would be able to heal the sick. This is what he writes:

> It speedily became apparent to the disciples that our Lord meant what He said when He assured them that they would do greater works than He had done. His miracles had amazed them and had done much good. And yet, after all, they were necessarily very limited in number, in the area of their exercise, and in the permanence of their results. . . .[5]
>
> These miracles were not acts terminating in themselves, and finding their full significance in the happiness communicated to the healed person; they were signs pointing to a power over men's spirits, and suggesting to men analogous but everlasting benefits. Christ wrought His miracles that men, beginning with what they could see and appreciate, might be led on to believe in and trust Him for power to help them in all their matters. And now He expressly announced to His disciples that these works which He had been doing were not works of the highest kind; that miracles of the highest kind were works of healing and renewal wrought not on the bodies but on the souls of men, works whose effects would not be deleted by disease and death, but would be permanent, works which should not be confined to Palestine, but should be co-extensive with the human race. And these greater works He would now proceed to accomplish through His disciples.

Of course, there is truth in what Marcus Dods says. But is that truth contained in the Scripture passage on which he comments? No doubt, the spiritual activities and accomplishments of the Church down through the ages are greater works than mere bodily cures. But why, by a subtle twist of exposition, leave the latter out completely? Certainly in this passage our Lord did not speak in the way suggested by His modern exponent. Moreover, if His "breath-taking promise" did refer to the disciples' power to accomplish great spiritual miracles, would not the greater include the less? Why not the healing of the body, as well as the healing of the soul? And if it be replied that the Johannine passage does not clearly indicate a healing ministry, it cannot be denied that in the Synoptic Gospels the Master's commission to His disciples to heal the sick is plainly marked.

With some writers the view that this aspect of the Church's ministry to human need was meant for the first generation of believers only is related to their Christological theory. In the laudable interest of safeguarding His uniqueness they trace the healing ministry of our Lord "not to His perfect manhood, which makes it possible for the Spirit of God to work through Him, but to His essential Godhead resuming as it were its Divine power and acting, as is the Divine way, creatively in the world of time and space."[6] Thus, a Scottish theologian already quoted writes: "Nothing could well be further from a true interpretation of Christ's purpose than that He meant to encourage the idea that now by the power of faith analogous to His own an epoch was dawning in which miracles would be at the service of humanity for the relief of physical woes. It is true, He empowered His disciples to work miracles, but it was as an equipment for their mission in proclaiming Himself, and it was subordinate to the spiritual purpose of the Kingdom.... There is ... no evidence that the power of working miracles or even of doing cures was inherent in discipleship as such, however much faith there might be.... The purpose of these miracles was, as in Christ's own, not so much to get the specific things done, as to testify that a supernatural person had appeared and claimed allegiance and faith. That testification was desirable for a certain period after Christ Himself, but it was plainly not necessary or desirable as a permanence."[7]

The same general point of view seems to underlie the statement of a well-known British psychologist, who states: "Jesus was a perfectly unique personality, and he had a perfectly unique mission to fulfil. That mission will never need to be carried out again; there never was and there never will be another Jesus. That being so, it is not unreasonable for anyone who believes in God at all, to expect that things would happen in relation to Jesus, which could never happen to any other person, before or since, not even to his own immediate disciples. And so they did, but that does not mean that Jesus was a magician, or independent of the nature of things. . . . Jesus did not class his miracles among his great works, and in many cases he took pains to secure secrecy about them. He did not base his claims on them; they were the spontaneous expressions of his compassionate spirit and his dynamic personality." And with special reference to the Johannine passage he says: "Whatever may have been meant by the saying about 'Greater works than these shall ye do,' I do not think it can be taken as referring to works of healing at all."[8]

A careful examination of these two passages will show that they are not on all fours. The theologian holds that the healing miracles of Jesus (and, of course, the nature miracles, too) bear witness to the Deity of Christ, and that their continuance in the Apostolic Church was allowed for the same purpose. The psychologist thinks that the healing miracles of Jesus reveal Him as a dynamic personality. He is not sure that they were repeated by the first generation of disciples, though he does say:

FAITH HEALING

"With regard to the miracles of the early Church, I should not violently oppose anyone who claimed, on general principles, that in the first days of Christianity the direct intervention of God in human affairs was more necessary and more frequent than it is today."[9] But his skepticism reveals itself in his added statement: "I am even more disposed than in the case of Jesus to seek for explanations of the apostles' miracles in natural terms, and to reject those which cannot be so explained."[9] To Dr. Yellowlees, Jesus is the Supreme Psychotherapist, who relied chiefly on suggestion for the cures He effected. To Dr. Porteous, Jesus is the Eternal Son of God, the Saviour of the World, whose healing miracles—as well as the nature miracles—were wrought in virtue of His Deity. But both agree on one point, that it was never the intention of the Master that the healing of the physically and mentally sick was to be part of the Church's permanent work for suffering humanity.

Each of the two positions outlined above raises an important question relative to the continuance of the healing miracles, though at bottom these two questions are really one. Of the Scottish theologian and those who favor his view of the cessation of miracles we ask: If it is possible to accept the healing miracles in the New Testament—and indeed the Biblical miracles generally—why is it unreasonable to believe that they have sometimes occurred in post-apostolic times and that they sometimes happen in our day? There does not seem to be any objection in principle to the continuance of such manifestations of God's power and love in any age, if they can occur in one. Why accept events which happened centuries ago and yet maintain that they do not, because they cannot, happen now? Is God's loving concern for His earthly children less now than it was at the beginning of the Christian era? And has His power to help in time of need diminished? Of course, it may be retorted that since miracles do not happen now the Church's ability to work them has been withdrawn. But that is a specious begging of the question, because it assumes that miracles no longer happen. Furthermore, it is argued that in New Testament times the healing miracles (and the nature miracles) were given to substantiate the saving truth that was being revealed in the Gospel of Christ, and that the guarantee of their truth is the fact that they are recorded in the Scriptures. But here again is a circle in the argument. The authority of the revelation secures the genuineness of the miracles, and the genuineness of the miracles guarantees the authority of the revelation.

A second question, closely related to the foregoing, is evoked by the position taken up by Dr. Yellowlees. He is strongly inclined to think that our Lord's healing miracles were just foreglimpses of the cures wrought by the techniques of modern medical psychology. But, with a curious inconsistency, he says that he would not violently object to the view that at the beginning of the Christian movement "the direct intervention of God in human affairs was more necessary and more frequent than it is today." This, however, is sheer assumption. What proof have we that it was more necessary then than it is now? Or that it was more frequent then than it is now? Does Dr. Yellowlees really believe that the healing miracles of Jesus represent "the direct intervention of God in human affairs"? If so, then he must also think of them as something above and beyond what he himself as a medical psychologist can accomplish. He gives the impression that he believes miracles do happen, but they are not so necessary or so frequent as in the days of Christ and His Apostles. Hence it would appear that if we are prepared to accept the miraculous element in the New Testament there is no insuperable obstacle in the way of believing that it could have continued in the affairs of men and in the life of the Church right down to the present age.

The Catholic Church (as we have seen previously) maintains that the healing miracles have not vanished from the religious life of Christendom, and that they have occurred again and again all down through the Christian centuries. Most Protestants would deny this, arguing that the need for spiritual cures passed away soon after the days of the Apostles. But today an increasing number of people—both inside and outside the major Protestant denominations—have come to believe that the necessity for these unusual demonstrations has never ceased, and that they are as much in evidence today as ever in the past. From this position the next step is easy to take: to believe that these demonstrations are given in healing meetings of all sorts and sizes, and at the various healing shrines of Europe and America. As we have seen, there is ample reason to hold that "miraculous" cures do take place; and this, to many people, is justification for urging that Protestantism recover its lost heritage and add to the preaching of the Gospel the healing of the sick—the sick in body and mind, as well as the sick in soul. The Reformation in the sixteenth century meant the rediscovery of the doctrine of justification by faith; a like genuine revival of spiritual religion in this twentieth century might mean the rediscovery of the practice of healing by faith.

10   Healing: the Way Forward

IT MAY BE that that revival is now taking place, or at least that we are on the verge of it. Some observers of the "signs of the times" affirm this confidently. They see marked indications that the power of God is descending on this generation and that this new spiritual impulse will reveal itself, amongst other things, in the healing of men's bodies and minds through the offices of a truly vitalized religion. Faith healers of the type of Oral Roberts and George Jeffries are constantly insisting upon this, and their spectacular successes—both in drawing huge congregations and in accomplishing many apparent cures —give them some right to do so. But over and above this is the testimony of the many clergy who take the ministry of intercession for the sick with real seriousness, who encourage their congregations to do so both in public worship and in prayer groups, and who as part of their Church's ministry to human need hold regular healing service in which the methods of the Apostolic Church are used more or less successfully.

But for this ministry of healing to become well grounded and truly effective—and especially to prevent its becoming a happy hunting ground for charlatans and quacks—two considerations must be implicated in practice. One is a thorough

FAITH HEALING

investigation into the mental and spiritual factors involved. The other is the close association of religion and medicine in the cure of human afflictions.

That there are, in this matter of faith healing, many difficult problems to be faced is obvious to all who know anything at all about the question. There is the problem of failures; and the related problem of the greater number of failures in relation to the number of cures than in the case of orthodox medical methods. For example, Christian Science claims many cures, but it also has many non-cures. And it might not be too hard to demonstrate the same thing where spectacular faith healing meetings are concerned. We have argued in a previous chapter that faith healing failures are in themselves no argument against the reality of faith healing successes, and more, that the fact that orthodox medicine has its failures is no reason for not going to the doctor. But many professional faith healers pay only lip service to the value of modern medicine, surgery and psychotherapy. They rarely say to their patients, "You need medical advice"; if ever they do tell a patient to go to the doctor, it is to show the doctor that a cure has been effected. There is real danger in bypassing medical help, and not a few men and women have died—and not a few parents have lost a child in death—because in relying upon some professional faith healer they have neglected or rejected outright what medical science has confidently to offer.

The fact of failure is a problem in the fields of both orthodox and unorthodox healing, but it is as a religious problem that it presses most heavily. Spiritual healers are apt to insist that there are no incurable diseases, and they like to point out that our Lord Himself never subscribed to the dictum: "This disease is incurable." Sometimes an older doctor today will tell a newcomer to medicine: "Never say a case is hopeless"; it is a reminder that the doctor's task is never finished until the patient's life is finished; and every experienced medico can tell of presumed hopeless cases which, for unknown reasons, have recovered. It may be that in the background spiritual forces have been at work—forces released by "the prayer of the righteous." But if the patient does die as the result of an ailment at present classed as incurable by known medical procedures, there is no problem save that of further research into the causes of the lethal complaint. But when the professional healer fails, a religious problem of the first order is involved. He will confidently proclaim that God wills that the patient should be healed, but when healing does not come the patient is made to believe that he lacks sufficient faith.

That faith is an important factor is profoundly true. But there have been saintly and devoted Christians of many years' standing whose faith is much bigger than the proverbial "grain of mustard seed" yet who have not been cured, whereas there have been people with no spiritual convictions and no religious faith to whom miraculous healing has come. It would seem that there are factors other than faith, and it may be that we do not yet know what those factors are. It may be that further experience will uncover them. They may be secondary to faith, so that the word of Christ still stands: "Thy faith hath saved thee," but though secondary they are nonetheless important, and must be fulfilled.

Furthermore, it is clear that spiritual healing must operate within the context of "natural law." The great English physician Sir Clifford Allbut has stated that we cannot set any limits to the power of faith healing, adding that "no limb, no viscus, is so far a vessel of dishonor as to be wholly outside the renewals of the spirit."[1] As medical testimony to the undeniable interaction of the body-mind and spirit it can be confidently accepted. But the noted physician would not like to be tied down too closely to his statement. How about an amputated limb, or a severed spinal cord, or a lost finger? Are these not beyond "the renewals of the spirit"? It would seem that even our Lord worked within the order of nature, when, for example, He fed the multitudes and healed the man with the withered arm. In the first case he used the loaves and fishes of a small boy; He did not wave His arm or speak a word that brought loaves of bread and pieces of broiled fish miraculously descending from heaven. And in the case of the man with the withered arm, if instead of being withered the arm had been missing, would a new arm have suddenly appeared out of nowhere at Christ's command?

Another consideration arises. There have been devoted servants of God afflicted with some complaint, intractable to orthodox medicine, but theoretically curable by faith, yet who have known the frustrating experience of unanswered prayer. Frances Ridley Havergal, the writer of that well-loved hymn

> Take my life, and let it be
> Consecrated, Lord, to Thee.

was a lifelong invalid. No doubt she prayed often and earnestly for healing, but it did not come; she died at the early age of forty-three. Again, take the great Apostle to the Gentiles. St. Paul had a grievous affliction that seriously hampered his Christian work. He was God's handicapped man. Here, if anywhere it seems that the Divine Healer should have intervened. But He did not—at least, not to remove the ailment. Whatever it was the Apostle suffered from—malaria, ophthalmia, curvature of the spine, a stammering tongue—it remained. Yet his agonizing prayers were not offered in vain, for

Healing: the Way Forward

> The answer he got to the prayer he made,
> Was power to see the thing through.

God did intevene, but not with a miraculous cure of the bodily ailment. St. Paul found himself "strengthened with might in the inner man." The Voice said, ". . . My grace is sufficient for thee: for my strength is made perfect in weakness. . . ." It was a tremendous spiritual experience which enabled the Apostle to exclaim enthusiastically, "Most gladly therefore will I rather glory in my infirmities, that the power of Christ may rest upon me" (II Corinthians 12:9). Perhaps there is a clue to the riddle here. While it is true that "His will is our health," it may be that for the sake of a larger purpose He lovingly permits some faithful servant to carry "without let-up" a heavy burden of suffering.

Furthermore, there is the fact of death. Says an old Turkish proverb: "Death is the black camel that kneels at every man's gate." We cannot escape it, however long delayed it may be. It comes to everyone sooner or later. Does it not follow then that in many cases sickness is not to be cured, but must end in that strange experience whereby we "shuffle off this mortal coil," and that God's ultimate healing is transition into the Life Eternal? Most Orthodox Christians are inclined to believe that if sin had not entered the world there would be no disease and no death; and certainly death in its spiritual aspects seems connected with the Fall of Man. There are some believers, however, who argue that disease and death as natural phenomena were present in the animal creation, independent of "man's first disobedience and the fall" (to borrow the phrase of John Milton). Of one thing we can be certain, that death plays a beneficent role in the economy of nature. Furthermore, we can see that in the world as we know it death is related to bodily and mental ills; it must therefore follow that finally all spiritual healing, as all physical and psychological healing, must end in failure. If we do not recognize these facts of life, then we are indeed living in a fool's paradise.

Modern medicine has increased man's life expectancy, and will continue to do so; and the genuine religious faith in the Father's loving purpose, the Son's saving grace, and the Holy Spirit's enabling power, can undergird and strengthen the believer's "will to live." The Biblical span of "threescore years and ten" may be extended into a century as the normal length of human life; it may go even higher. But there is a limit to what medical science can do for us in this respect; and in the Gospel of Christ there is nothing to suggest that even the most faith-filled believer can hope to live forever on "this terrestrial ball." Through a true alliance of science and religion, meeting "the last enemy" may eventually be delayed for most people, but ultimately the battle is joined, and the "dark invader" triumphs. Even Methuselah had to die at last.

No one will deny that modern medicine has indeed prolonged man's earthly span. The testimony of vital statistics, and the achievements of the public health services in preventing epidemics, are ample proof of this. But what about spiritual healing in this respect? Sir Henry Cohen, past president of the British Medical Association, declared that "modern ailments cannot be measured by the stethoscope alone; the symptoms may be the thumping heart, the cold sweat, the weak and tremulous knees of fright, but the causes are likely enough a man's loves and hates, his passions and fears, his worries and anxieties." These negative and destructive emotions cannot be cured by the physician's drugs or the surgeon's knife. Psychotherapy, it is true, can deal with some of these "emotional warps," but if the testimony of such outstanding psychiatrists as C. G. Jung and James A. Hadfield (quoted in earlier pages)

Healing: the Way Forward

is to be relied upon—and why not?—then the only sure remedy is a vital trust in the power and grace of God.

Sixty years ago William James wrote: "The sovereign cure for worry is religious faith." He would say it even more emphatically today. Indeed, he would proclaim that the sovereign cure for all these destructive emotional twists is a genuine religious faith. G. K. Chesterton used to say that Protestants have substituted the psychoanalyst's couch for the priest's confessional box; and it is generally agreed that far fewer Catholics than non-Catholics resort to the psychotherapist. That could well be an indirect testimony to the therapeutic value of religion. Certainly it may be affirmed that vital religion helps men not only to live better but also to live longer, and therefore that it, too, has made a contribution to lengthening the span of human existence.

It is the function of the Church as a whole to create vital religion in the hearts of men, but there are some outstanding individuals in the Church who seem to possess in a marked degree the ability to make their fellows realize the power and grace of God. They have had bestowed upon them what in the New Testament is claimed as one of the "gifts of the Holy Spirit," the gift of healing. In the modern Church this gift is not confined to any sacred caste; it is not the exclusive possession of "holy men" or of those ordained in the supposedly proper manner. Members of the clergy and of the laity appear to have this gift, and it overleaps denominational boundaries. Very often the people who possess this gift of healing, and are thus able to exercise this charismatic (as it is called) ministry to the sick, are very simple in faith and understanding. They may have little in the way of educational background, and may even be afflicted with much intellectual and theological confusion—though they may not be conscious of it as an affliction. But they have something deeper than the gifts of intellect. They have spiritual intuition, and the power to make come true today the words that we sometimes sing about the Healing Christ:

> Thy touch has still its ancient power,
> No word from Thee can fruitless fall.

There seems to rest upon them a "double portion" of Christ's spirit, and thus they are able to perform those "greater works" to which we have previously referred. They are truly consecrated men and women. We feel in their presence that they habitually move on a higher plane of spiritual existence than that of the average Christian, and are thus able to contact and channel spiritual resources that are beyond the reach of the vast majority of us.

We can sum up the foregoing pages by saying that religion and medicine are both involved in the healing of men's afflictions. The recognition of this fact calls for a deeper understanding and a closer cooperation between ministers and doctors. Indeed, the way forward in the conquest of disease lies here. There seems to be some Scriptural warrant for such cooperation (James 5:14), even though modern medical techniques have far outdistanced the ancient procedure of anointing with oil. In our day it will mean that doctors will have to be more religious and ministers will have to be more scientific. There are obstacles—but not insuperable ones—on both sides. If an individual doctor—be he physician or surgeon or psychotherapist—is a thoroughgoing materialist, with no conviction as to the reality of spiritual values, he is not likely to seek, or to accept if offered, the help of minister, priest, or rabbi in the healing of a sick person. And if the official representative of religion is crudely unscientific in his approach to the problem of

Healing: the Way Forward

sickness even the most spiritually-minded doctor will be loath to work with him. The doctor must realize that medicine is not a substitute for religion, and the minister must understand that religion is no substitute for medicine. The respective spheres in which these two "servants of the most high God" operate are not rivals, but neither are they identical. Of course, they overlap in the realm of healing, but each makes its distinctive contribution, and they must not be confused. The offices of religion cannot take the place of the physician's drugs, the surgeon's knife, or the analyst's couch, but neither can these healing techniques take the place of intercessory prayer and sacramental worship.

Doctors and clergy can work together as individuals, and there are many cases in which they do. They can also get together in groups for further cooperative study and mutual helpfulness, and again there are cases in which they do. And of such joint efforts we can say, adapting a saying of our common Lord: "Let both *work* together until the harvest"—the harvest being a world in which men can live happier and longer lives, free from the sicknesses which now afflict them. Disease will be no more. And neither will death be any more. For what we in this disease-infested world know as death will become what the New Testament calls a "falling on sleep"—life closing in the twilight and opening again in the morning.

NOTES

CHAPTER 1

1. C. G. Jung, *Modern Man in Search of a Soul* (New York, Harcourt, Brace and Company, Inc., 1933), p. 264. It may be unnecessary to remark that Dr. Jung, first a disciple and then a rival of Sigmund Freud, was the leading authority in his own field. He was the founder of what is called "analytical psychology."
2. The Book of Job was written to refute this exaggerated doctrine. Although some suffering is the result of wickedness, a righteous man may be afflicted despite his innocence—a truth that the experience of Job is intended to illustrate and prove.
3. The story of King Asa (II Chronicles 16) seems to suggest this. Asa "was diseased in his feet . . . yet in his disease he sought not to the Lord, but to the physicians." The implications of the story are that Asa's affliction was the result of sin, and that instead of repenting of his wickedness, he went to the physicians for a cure—behind God's back, as it were.
4. G. G. Dawson, *Healing: Pagan and Christian* (New York, The Macmillan Company, 1935), p. 90n. Dr. Dawson's volume, first published in 1935, is a very competent review of the whole subject of healing in its various aspects.
5. The Book of Ecclesiasticus, 38:1-15. This work, which in the quoted passage pays such a discriminating and graceful tribute to the medical profession, is an apocryphal writing not included in our Bible. It was written about 180 B.C. by Jesus ben Sirach, and is replete with the ripe experience of a fine man who "saw life steadily and saw it whole."

CHAPTER 2

1. Adolf von Harnack, *The Expansion of Christianity* (London, Williams & Norgate, Ltd., 1904), I, 101.

Notes

2. Dr. Leslie D. Weatherhead must be placed in this category, as witness his explanation of such "miracles" as the stilling of the tempest and the withering of the barren fig tree. See his *When the Lamp Flickers* (Nashville, Abingdon Press, 1948), p. 64f. It must be added, however, that Dr. Weatherhead emphatically believes in Christ's healing miracles.

3. Matthew Arnold's dogmatic statement, "Miracles do not happen," invites the apt rejoinder, "Then it is a miracle if they do not."

4. *God and the Bible* (London, Smith, Elder & Co., Ltd., 1875), p. 23.

5. Sir John Seeley, *Ecce Homo* (London, J. M. Dent & Sons, Ltd., 1907), p. 41.

6. H. G. Wood, "The Life and Teaching of Jesus Christ," *Peake's Commentary on the Bible* (Edinburgh, Thomas Nelson & Sons, Ltd.), p. 663.

7. Seeley, *op. cit.*, p. 177.

8. Hugh Gainsborough and Eliot Slater, "A Study of Peptic Ulcer," *British Medical Journal* (August 24, 1946), as quoted in Leslie D. Weatherhead, *Psychology, Religion, and Healing* (Nashville, Abingdon Press, 1951), p. 40. See also p. 20.

9. G. Simpson Marr, *Christianity and the Cure of Disease*, p. 29. See also Leslie D. Weatherhead, *His Life and Ours* (Nashville, Abingdon Press, 1931), pp. 156-157.

10. D. S. Cairns, *The Faith That Rebels* (New York, Harper & Brothers, 1928), p. 169.

11. *Ibid.*, pp. 16-17.

12. *Psychology, Religion, and Healing*, pp. 90-91. The authority Weatherhead quotes is William Menzies Alexander, *Demonic Possession in the New Testament: Its Relations, Historical, Medical and Theological* (Edinburgh, T.&T. Clark, 1902), p. 50.

13. From *Proceedings of the American Society for Psychic Research*, III, 586, as quoted in Elwood Worcester, *Making Life Better* (New York, Charles Scribner's Sons, 1936), p. 45.

NOTES

14. *The Life of Christ,* pp. 148-149, as quoted in Elwood Worcester and Samuel McComb, *Body, Mind and Spirit* (New Hampshire, Marshall Jones & Co., 1931), p. 272. These authors assert, on the same page, that "there are today educated and skilled physicians who believe in obsession by an extraneous intelligence and whose therapeutic system is based on this conviction."

15. *Psychology, Religion, and Healing,* p. 89. "This light-hearted way" means, of course, the summary dismissal of the demon-possession theory as sheer error.

CHAPTER 3

1. L. W. Grensted, "Psychology and God" (*Bampton Lectures for 1930*), p. 100.
2. *His Life and Ours,* pp. 157-158. Dr. Weatherhead wisely remarks, "Of course, the difficulty is that we do not know what conditions of mind in the woman made that possible, and how they can be produced in another. Obviously, it would be cruel to deduce that the treatment which worked then is to be recommended to cancer patients everywhere."
3. A placebo is a harmless concoction—a colored sugar pill, a starch capsule, a pleasant tasting liquid, or a sterile water injection—prescribed by doctors to bolster up the morale, and so help the patient to recover. It is often a successful healing device. But behind the patient's acceptance of the alleged medicine there is always faith in his physician. Otherwise, the placebo is likely to be a failure.
4. A. C. Turner, "Faith, Prayer and the World's Order," *Concerning Prayer,* ed. B. H. Streeter (New York, The Macmillan Co., 1922), p. 403.
5. I heard a minister preach a sermon on prayer, based on references to the subject in the Epistle of James. But he studiously avoided all mention of the place of prayer in the healing of the

Notes

sick; he made not the slightest reference to the most important passage in the epistle. As far as he was concerned James 5:13-16 might never have been written. His neglect is all the more remarkable in that he himself was just recovering from a heart attack!

6. Raynor C. Johnson, *The Imprisoned Splendor* (London, Hodder & Stoughton, Ltd., 1953), p. 260.

7. H. H. Farmer, *The World and God* (London, James Nisbet & Co., Ltd., 1935), p. 122.

8. Among the best-known of these are the Cathedral Church of St. Luke, Philadelphia, Pa.; St. Peter's Episcopal Church, Brentwood, Pittsburgh, Pa.; Mount Vernon Place Methodist Church, Baltimore, Md.; and Cavendish Congregational Church, Manchester, England. I have noticed that at Healing Services about 90 per cent of the congregation, and of those who come forward for prayer and the laying on of hands, are women. Does this signify the ratio of sickness as between the sexes? Or does it mean that women are more ready than men to believe in spiritual healing?

9. Johnson, *loc. cit.*

10. For example, during the lifetime of the great Roman Catholic missionary, St. Francis Xavier, no miracles were claimed for him, either by himself or by his missionary companions. After his death at least a dozen striking miracles were attributed to him, including making salt water fresh, causing an earthquake, burying a town under ashes, inducing a crab to restore a crucifix lost at sea, and even raising the dead. Many miracles were ascribed to St. Thomas à Becket of Canterbury. Some of them were healing, such as the cure of leprosy; others were "nature miracles," such as turning Canterbury water into milk. See H. E. Fosdick, *The Modern Use of the Bible* (New York, The Macmillan Co., 1924), p. 143f.

CHAPTER 4

1. It is interesting to compare this with Oral Roberts' claim that, in answer to prayer, God healed him of tuberculosis and

NOTES

stammering, and commissioned him to undertake his healing campaign.

2. A therapeutic device currently insisted upon, with much popular success, by Dr. Norman Vincent Peale.
3. "One Night—And Forever," *Guideposts*, August, 1953.
4. Chief among these medical men was Dr. Isadore Coriat, who collaborated with the two clergymen in writing an important pioneer work, *Religion and Medicine* (New York, Moffat, Yard & Co., 1908).
5. Pp. vi, xiii-xiv. These words were written a quarter of a century after the Emmanuel Movement began.
6. Guild of Health Leaflet No. 1.
7. Dr. Weatherhead deals, in some detail, with these various societies in *Psychology, Religion, and Healing,* Section III, Chap. VI.
8. *A Doctor Heals by Faith* (London, Max Parrish & Co., Ltd., 1953), p. 37.

CHAPTER 5

1. Alexis Carrel, *Man, the Unknown* (New York, Harper & Brothers, 1939), as quoted by Woodard, *A Doctor Heals by Faith*, p. 51.
2. Weatherhead, *Psychology, Religion, and Healing,* p. 509f.
3. Howard Somervell, *After Everest* (London, Hodder & Stoughton, Ltd., 1953), p. 274f.
4. Sherwood Eddy, *You Will Survive After Death* (New York, Rinehart & Co., Inc., 1950), p. 88f. Mr. Parrish became a leading "psychic-healer," but it is not necessary to accept the spiritualistic hypothesis to believe in the reality of his spiritual cures.
5. Elsie H. Salmon, *He Heals Today* (Evesham, Arthur James, Ltd., 1951), p. 129f.
6. Grensted, "Psychology and God" (*Bampton Lectures for 1930*) p. 113.
7. It is worth noting that McDougall's first book was *A Primer of Physiological Psychology*.

Notes

8. Erwin G. Liek, *Miracle in the Art of Healing*, as quoted in *The Transformation of the Scientific World View* (New York, Harper & Brothers, 1954), p. 184. Karl Heim gives this further passage from Liek: "Zeileis, a famous healer at Galspach, near Linz, cured cases of tuberculosis, cancer, epilepsy, diabetes, arteriosclerosis, blindness and paralysis. It is clear, therefore, that it is not merely 'nervous' but also organic illness, i.e., not merely psychopathic functional disturbance, but also anatomical afflictions which are open to be influenced in psychic ways" (p. 179).

9. *The New York Times*, April 8, 1956.

10. E. L. H. Ash, *Faith and Suggestion* (London, Herbert & Daniel, Ltd., 1912), as quoted in Harold Anson, "Prayer and Bodily Health," *Concerning Prayer*, ed. B. H. Streeter, p. 339n.

11. *Psychology, Religion, and Healing*, pp. 244-245.

12. "The Psychology of Power," *The Spirit*, ed. B. H. Streeter (London, Macmillan, Ltd., 1919), p. 113f. Cf. Dr. Weatherhead's testimony: "I once heard a specialist say that the balance between life and death was often tilted down on the side of life by the timely visit of the right kind of minister" (*Psychology, Religion, and Healing*, p. 478).

CHAPTER 6

1. *An Enquiry Concerning Human Understanding*, Section X.

2. *Miracles* (New York, The Macmillan Co., 1947), p. 15. Dr. Lewis admits that he uses this definition as a concession to popular ideas on the subject, claiming that it enables him "most easily to treat those questions which 'the common reader' probably has in mind when he takes up a book on Miracles."

3. H. E. Fosdick, *The Modern Use of the Bible* (New York, The Macmillan Co., 1924), p. 161.

4. Alan Richardson, *Christian Apologetics* (London, Student Christian Movement Press Limited, 1947), pp. 150-155.

NOTES

5. "Nature, Man and God," *Gifford Lectures,* 1932-33, 1933-34, p. 27.
6. "The Gospel for an Age of Doubt," p. 257.
7. This parable appeared many years ago in a now defunct theological magazine. It is, I think, worth preserving. The author was the famous English theologian and expositor of the Victorian era, Dr. Samuel Cox.
8. Johannes Wendland, *Miracles and Christianity* (London Hodder & Stoughton, Ltd.), p. 1.
9. John Porteous, *Order and Grace* (London, James Clarke & Co., Ltd.), p. 241.

CHAPTER 7

1. J. B. Rhine, *The New World of the Mind* (New York, William Sloane Associates, 1953), p. 25. Dr. Rhine is the famous psychologist at Duke University. He succeeded his brilliant master, William McDougall, and inherited his interest in parapsychology.
2. Charles Baudouin, *Suggestion and Auto-Suggestion* (London, Allen & Unwin, Ltd., 1920), p. 26. What Coué called the subconscious, Freud and his disciples call "the unconscious," by which is meant the inaccessible region below the level of consciousness into which painful emotions and experiences are automatically repressed by the waking mind. The contents of the unconscious are not recoverable by the ordinary processes of remembering—only by psychoanalytical methods, such as hypnotism, dream-analysis, word association tests, etc.
3. As quoted in Weatherhead, *Psychology, Religion, and Healing,* p. 204.
4. *Ibid.,* p. 144.
5. F. W. H. Myers, *Human Personality, and Its Survival of Bodily Death* (New York, Longmans, Green & Co., Inc., 1954, reprint), as quoted in W. F. Cobb, *Spiritual Healing,* p. 119.

Notes

CHAPTER 8

1. These, of course, are intercessory prayer, laying on of hands, anointing, the mass revival meeting, and dipping in a sacred pool (as at Lourdes), etc.
2. *Man, the Unknown,* p. 145.
3. Oliver Cromwell was accustomed to say that "to be a seeker is to be in the next best sect to being a finder." A greater than Cromwell said, "Seek and ye shall find."
4. Nothing could be more mystifying than the "miracle of sight," but we do not feel the mystery because we take seeing for granted. Hypnotism mystifies because it is far less common.
5. *Instinct and the Unconscious* (London, Cambridge University Press, 1922), p. 183.
6. Quoted in Grensted, "Psychology and God" (*Bampton Lectures for 1930*), p. 116.
7. This is the definition of the noted American philosopher, Josiah Royce. It is quoted in E. Stanley Jones, *Christ and Human Suffering* (Nashville, Abingdon Press, 1933), p. 141.
8. C. P. Martin, *The Decline of Religion* (London, Allen & Unwin, Ltd., 1940), p. 162. Despite its title, this remarkable book, by the professor of anatomy at McGill University, Montreal, is a brilliant defense of the Christian faith by a first-class scientist.

CHAPTER 9

1. The other five are: "I am the light of the world"; "I am the door"; "I am the way, the truth, and the life"; "I am the good shepherd"; and "I am the vine."
2. *The Expansion of Christianity,* as quoted in Cairns, *The Faith That Rebels,* p. 21.
3. Porteous, *op. cit.,* p. 175.
4. *The Interpreter's Bible* (Nashville, Abingdon Press, 1952), VIII, 705-706.

NOTES

5. "The Gospel of John," *Expositor's Bible,* ed. W. Robertson Nicoll, (Grand Rapids, William B. Eerdmans Publishing Co.), II, 145-146.
6. Cairns, *The Faith That Rebels,* p. 30.
7. Porteous, *op. cit.,* pp. 173-174.
8. David Yellowlees, *Psychology's Defence of the Faith* (London, Student Christian Movement Press Limited), pp. 180-181.
9. *Ibid.,* p. 184.

CHAPTER 10

1. Quoted in W. F. Cobb, "Faith Healing," *Encyclopedia of Religion and Ethics,* ed. James Hastings (New York, Charles Scribner's Sons, 1951), VI, 701.